The Intuit

The Intuit

April Dawn Corbitt

ISBN: 978-0-578-44301-0

Dedication

This book is dedicated to the human race. May we all recognize our magnitude as BEINGS!

Acknowledgments

❖

THERE ARE REALLY NO WORDS to describe my appreciation for so many individuals who played a role in my writing this book. I have no idea where to begin, and this order has nothing to do with the level of appreciation I have, because without even the smallest gesture, this book would not be.

- *My parents.* You raised me to be a fearless teacher. I could not have chosen better parents to groom me to understand the power and effect that believing thoughts can have. You did everything you were supposed to do, and I love you with all of my *being*!
- *My son.* You have been the greatest gift in my life. The word "love" just falls short when it comes to how much you mean to me. You are brilliant, and I love watching you step into your power more and more every day. Your big, beautiful, overflowing heart is so unique. You are a true gift to this world.

- *Dennis.* Without you I probably would never have stepped into my intuition. The love, support, and encouragement you have *endlessly* given me gave me a beautiful platform to step into who I was as a *being*. No words of gratitude could even come close to what I feel inside.
- *Karen* (a.k.a.: soul sister). Thank you for your friendship, support, and encouragement. Thank you for believing in me, teaching me, writing the medical terminology in this book, and showing me what true, unconditional love looks like.
- *Martha.* In ways you taught me how to write because we just kept trying. I had no clue how to get the information inside me out, and for a long time, only a bunch of crap came out of me. You didn't give up on me, and we kept at it until I was able to fly on my own and write this book.
- *Jessica.* Another soul sister! You never turned your back on me, even when I was a crazy person. You loved me and stood by me without judgment as I went through hell and back. For that I am eternally grateful.
- *Mia.* Another soul sister! Your endless support of this industry and of me should be revered. I love watching you flutter around with enthusiasm, constantly teaching.
- *Dimaris and Arthur.* Thank you for opening up your home to me so I could finish this book.

- *Mia, Dimaris, and Karen.* Thank you all for *hours* of editing and amazing comments that helped me round out this material.
- *Scooter (my dog).* You kept me alive and made me go out for walks when I didn't even want to breathe. You truly have been a best friend. My love!
- *Gavlin.* Without you I would never have faced my inner demons. Without you I would never have researched PTSD the way I did. Without you I would not be who I am today.
- *My guides.* Without all of you, I would not be here, know the things that I do, or be as strong as I am! Thank you!

Prologue:
Karen's Voice

⚜

I HAVE BEEN BLESSED IN my life to be a physician and to know and collaborate with an amazing intuit, April Dawn Corbitt. After working with April over the last ten years, I am convinced that she is one of the most accurate and brilliant intuits today. I have watched her uncover her intuition and develop her understanding of who we are as human beings and how our thoughts and beliefs create emotions that are woven into our cell tissue, creating physical symptoms and disease. Her intuitive ability to read the physical body and emotional body is more accurate than most of the medical tests I have at my disposal. She has gone beyond the mind knowledge of who we are as physical, emotional, and spiritual beings to reveal how we can get out of time and release the emotions from the cell tissue to heal from disease and suffering. Being with April on this incredible journey over the last ten years has changed my understanding of health and disease and opened new possibilities into true healing.

I believe all physicians use their intuition in caring for patients. We "know" when someone is sick or not, and we "sense" when a patient presenting with chest pain is really having a heart attack versus suffering from anxiety. However, Western medicine falls short in teaching and training younger physician how to access their own intuition and to use their impressions in caring for patients. While working with April, I am learning to trust my own intuition or inner knowing more every day. Now when we work together, she is teaching me how to sense and read a patient's physical and emotional body before I have any tests to confirm my impressions. I am continually amazed at my accuracy and now understand that we all are intuitive—our awareness of it varies from person to person. I know I am only touching the tip of the iceberg. She is correct in that we are all powerful intuitive beings, and just having simple awareness of our own intuition will start our journey down this wonderful path.

We currently rely more on lab tests, advance imaging scans, and genetic testing than I ever learned about going through medical school thirty years ago. Our advances in medical technology are constantly changing, yet our innate ability to sense our connectedness to another human being has never changed. We have forgotten how to listen—how to listen to our own "gestalt." I believe the future of medicine will place enormous value on intuition even more than medical technology. One day teaching and using intuition will be part of every medical school curriculum, and medical intuitives will be treasured parts of the patient-care teams. The human body, the mind, our beliefs, and emotions are so beautifully woven into a complex web of health and disease; we truly are magnificent beings. I know that one day, we will master our beliefs and emotions, and diseases and "dis-ease" in the physical body along with suffering will fall away. Perfect health can be a reality.

April is a powerful teacher and leader and will move this field forward as we enter a new paradigm of health, healing, and consciousness. Her purpose and passion to release human consciousness from suffering is truly inspiring. One day science will catch up with April as we research how our beliefs change our physical DNA and our emotions are stuck in our cell tissue. For now, she will forge forward, breaking down our barriers to understanding ourselves as intuitive beings.

April's journey beautifully detailed in *The Intuit* is both painful and joyous as you watch her wake up to her amazing intuitive being. Her darkest nights and brilliant, clear insights will inspire you to peel the layers off your own story and become aware of your own magnificence and intuitive abilities. Enjoy!

—Dr. Karen Van Hoesen
Clinical Professor, Emergency Medicine
University of California San Diego

As the story goes...

CHAPTER 1

In the Beginning...

❧

As Dr. Karen Van Hoesen and I made our way around the hospital emergency department (ED) seeing patients, I had a strong urge to go see a man in the triage area. Triage is where the nurses review patients' symptoms, determine levels of health severity, and check them in. Once the patients are brought back and put in ED rooms, Dr. Karen and I go to see them. But on this day, I was very drawn to go see this man.

I asked Karen, "Can we go see the guy up there?" motioning toward triage. Triage was about thirty feet further down the hallway. I could feel a man but couldn't see him because of the privacy curtain.

Without hesitation she said, "Sure!" And off we went to triage. As soon as we entered, several nurses asked Dr. Karen what she needed because they are not use to seeing doctors in this area unless there was an emergency or they needed something. Dr. Karen expressed that she just wanted to check on the patient. Behind the curtain sat a man in his fifties. The nurse told Dr. Karen that the patient was having chest tightness and shortness of breath. As they talked I wasn't really listening to their conversation. I could see the patient's name and age on the nurse's computer screen, and immediately I started to get impressions and sensations.

I saw an X-ACTO knife cutting through his heart. It showed me this round dark ball causing pressure and creating an exact line slicing through the heart. Once Dr. Karen and I were out of earshot, I said, "This man is going to die if what I see continues to happen." I described my impressions to her and explained that if what I see continued, it would rupture his heart, and he would die within a minute or two.

Now, please realize, I am not an overly dramatic person in the ED. At this point in time, I had already been doing research with Dr. Karen for ten years, and in all of that time, I had *never*, not once, said to her, "This person is going to die!" The ED is nothing like what you see on television shows. People are not coding constantly and being rushed into surgery. There are a lot of broken bones, head trauma, mental disorders, overdoses...but 99 percent of the time, they are not dying right then and there.

After hearing my impressions, Dr. Karen immediately had the man brought back and put in a bed, and she told the resident (this hospital is a teaching hospital) to go see him immediately. She ordered a STAT CT scan and blood work. Forty-five minutes later, the resident doctor rushed up to us and stated the patient's diagnosis. At the same time, Dr. Karen received a phone call from the radiologist due to the critical, abnormal findings on the CT scan.

If you were attending a lecture with Dr. Karen and me, I would hand it over to her at this point to describe in medical terms what was happening to this man. What I can tell you first is that the CT film looked *exactly* like my impressions, with a line slicing through the man's heart.

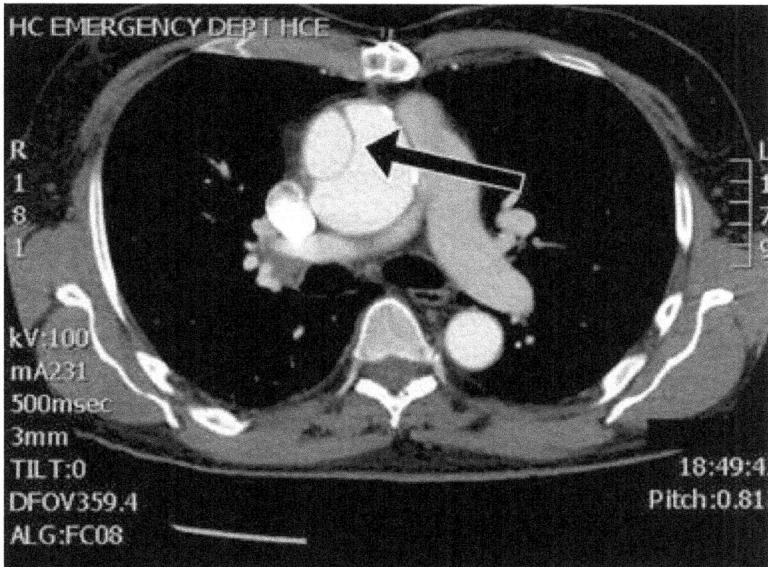

Here is what Karen has explained in live lectures.

"As soon as we walked into the triage area, the nurse handed me the patient's electrocardiogram (EKG). The EKG was normal; he was not having a heart attack. I asked him about his symptoms, and he described very nonspecific chest pain and was in no distress. *He would have been placed back in the waiting room until a bed was open and ready.* When April told me she saw an X-ACTO knife cutting through the patient's heart, that it was bulging and felt like it was going to rupture, she was describing an aortic dissection. An aortic dissection occurs when the wall of the aorta splits apart, creating two channels of blood flow, which weakens the wall, and the aorta can rupture. If that happens, the patient will loose blood into the chest cavity and can quickly die. *April has NO medical training*; she has never seen a CT scan of an aortic dissection or even knows what happens when the wall of the aorta separates. Yet I trusted her impression! We rushed the patient back to a bed in the ED, and I called radiology for a STAT CT scan, which did confirm what April was seeing: the wall of the aorta was separating. We called cardiothoracic surgery, and he was quickly transferred up to the operating room. He did well; this was one of those moments when April's impression was so exact that I acted much more rapidly and made the diagnosis quickly."

No, this is not a fiction book! The story above is a *true* story. At this point, most people want to ask me something like, "When did you first start to see things or know you were intuitive?"

I've pondered this question many times because there was no exact moment—like in a video game where I received a level-up or treasure box containing psychic abilities. There are moments I can remember I realized things. I developed it, and I removed blocks that stood in my way of sensing it, but there was not an exact moment. It's like my arm; it has always been there. It would be like me asking you when did you start to smell with your nose? You might at some point have realized you can smell, *but it was always there.*

The best way I've found to teach intuition is to just tell my story. As I do, most people relate and start to notice (become aware) that they have the same sensations. Once the awareness of *what it feels like* is there, you can start to work with it and develop it, similar to a singing voice or muscle memory.

Please know that at first, the things I'm telling you about my life may seem unnecessary or even hard to read. But as the book goes on, you will see why what I'm sharing is so important and pertinent to developing intuition.

Developing my intuition has been a very long, curvy road. I was not raised by some psychic grandmother who handed down all of her secrets, tools, and tricks of the trade, so to speak. No actually, I was born at home forty-two years ago, delivered by my dad. I have two older brothers. My mom's side of the family lived in separate houses on her parents' (my grandparents') large, beautiful farm in Arkansas. The grandkids all grew up together, rode the school bus together, played, fought, and did chores together. We moved away from the farm many times because my dad was bound and determined to get us off that farm and into a different way of life, but we kept returning to our house there for various reasons. When I was fourteen, my mom, dad, and I moved to California. After that, for most of my life, I have lived in California.

My family were/are Jehovah's Witnesses. (Again, I'm going to say what I've already said because numerous people who have edited this book want to take out important details of my story that are hard to digest, but if I take these parts out, then you will not understand what my base story [programming] was that stood in the way of me feeling/hearing my intuition!) My family taught me the belief that there is *no* life after death. They taught me that when you die, it is like you are sleeping with no consciousness at all. When Adam and Eve sinned, they lost perfection and eternal life. Jesus bought that back for us with his sacrifice of death. Someday Armageddon would come and wipe away all the people who did not serve Jehovah (their name for God). Then a paradise earth would be created, and the people who had died prior to Armageddon but who had loved Jehovah would be resurrected into the paradise earth. If you were talking to someone on the "other side" (no longer in physical form), Witnesses believe you are talking to demons.

When I was around eleven years old, I had this experience while sitting in my parents' bedroom. At the time, I did not understand what was happening, but looking back I understand now. The pictures on my parents' wall started to move within my mind's eye gently back and forth. I had always felt what I had labeled imaginary friends, but this day I was playing with something and ignoring my "imagination." I could see the pictures moving. I sensed this energetic *being* trying to get my attention without me looking at the wall. Although it did not hurt me, its insistence scared me, and I screamed for my parents. They came rushing into their bedroom. When I told them what I felt, of course it scared them, and they thought there was a demon in the house. After hours of them contemplating how this demon could have gotten in the house, they decided it was in a doll that had been given to me. The next day my dad took the doll and burned it. I was devastated. I loved that doll. He came home to report that it was really hard to burn and that a demon must have been in it trying to save it. What I didn't tell them was that none of the imaginary friends had gone away. I was too scared that they would burn more of my dolls. I now realize that so much of what I was seeing and experiencing, I labeled as my imagination because that was safe.

My parents taught me a lot of foundational thoughts about punishment, not enough, being an imperfect sinner, and the dream of a paradise earth if we lived through Armageddon. I'm sure you can imagine the kind of life that would be built on that kind of foundation.

At sixteen I was what they call a regular pioneer in the congregation of Jehovah's Witnesses. This meant I would go from door to door preaching at least ninety hours a month. I truly wanted to please Jehovah and my parents. This is how much I believed what I had been taught as a child. I was hurting inside and felt like, regardless of what I did, I wasn't good enough, nor did I fit in anywhere. I just seemed different, no matter how hard I tried. Back then I believed the tenets of the Jehovah's Witnesses because those were the only thoughts I had been around or had been taught.

I discredited my intuition by labeling it imagination or coincidence. One time when I was around fourteen, I was sitting on my bedroom floor drawing, and a woman manifested in front of me. What I mean by "manifested" is that I could feel her standing there, similar to feeling that someone is in the room with you when the lights are off. I could see her in my mind's eye; it was the way she showed herself to me. By "mind's eye," I mean, if I were to ask you what the house you live in looks like or the house you grew up in looks like, you can see an image of it within your mind. This is the same way and place in which we see things intuitively. So I could see her in my mind's eye and hear her within my mind. By saying "hear her within my mind," I'm referring to what occurs when you replay a conversation you have already had with someone within your mind. You can even hear the tone of the person's voice, but you are not hearing it through your ears. I could hear her as a conversation within my mind. (Again, at this point, I had labeled this my imagination.) She said something like, "You are a prophetess." I could hear her, but I kept drawing. I thought in my head, "That sounds unfun." She was very calm and kept standing there. After a while, I decided if she wanted to hang out with me or play with me, then I wanted to be a Power Ranger—the purple one, in fact! I laugh now thinking about this story and about how amused at me she must have been when I announced that. She did kind of laugh and tried to explain to me that I could see the waves of time. I could see the alignment of the stars. I don't remember exactly what she said to me because I was not interested in my imaginary friends' suggestion to play prophetess. I remember my mom calling me down for dinner, and off I went, not realizing what I had seen, heard, or been told.

I only went through the eighth grade, and much of my schooling had been home schooling. I was amazing at teaching people about the Jehovah's Witnesses' beliefs, and at that time I dedicated my life to that. My parents really taught me how to be a teacher, and I'm so grateful for that now.

My parents educated us as we lived. My dad was a general contractor, and from the time I could walk, I went to job sites with him. By the time I was fourteen, I could draw partial blueprints and was a very good finish carpenter. I loved building and working with my hands. My mom was an amazing cook. I always knew when she was stressed because she would cook everything in the house. I got that from her. Cooking is wonderful therapy for me. When I was very young, my mom worked in labor and delivery at the hospital and taught Lamaze classes. I remember learning Lamaze at around four years old. Learning to breathe deeply helped me in so many situations throughout life. Then my mom went back to school when I was fourteen for an accounting degree. She taught me as she learned, and I would help her with her clients. She would also help my dad with all his cost accounting for his construction jobs. By the time I was sixteen, I had my own accounting construction clients. Our education was received not so much in school but in the trenches, learning right beside them. My dad had only gone through the eighth grade, and he would always tell me, "It's not important how much schooling you have but how hard you work, how sincere you are! You can learn anything if you're teachable." I know that believing those thoughts created my success in the corporate world because I did work hard and was a very sincere person, willing to learn anything. Not knowing did not scare me because I knew I could learn.

Also, when I was 16, my oldest brother became a distributor for a company that created and sold accounting software. Once he had sold the software, I would then go in and help the company set up their accounting records and workflow. This started me on a very long and successful career. But I don't want to jump too far ahead just yet.

When I was seventeen, my parents moved to Palm Springs, California, but I wanted to stay in San Diego, so I moved in with a family that had a daughter only a few months older than me at the time, and she was also a regular pioneer. This was the start of my struggle with the beliefs of the Jehovah's Witnesses. For several reasons I started to question some of the beliefs, but questioning the brothers in the congregation or their beliefs is not something that is done in this organization. I talked to a woman friend of mine because I truly wanted to understand and didn't want to be a bad person. She told her husband, and the brothers from the congregation asked to talk to me after a meeting about the things I had said. I felt scared because I didn't want to get in trouble or be shunned, so I withdrew further and felt even more confused.

I felt this very strong desire to get my GED, so I started taking review classes when I was seventeen and a half. As soon as I turned eighteen, I took and passed the test for my GED and then started to take accounting courses through the local adult school.

At eighteen, I decided to move to Palm Springs, California, where my parents were living. There I met a brother in the congregation. We will call him Trout. Our relationship gave me a false sense of belonging and purpose. He was also struggling with the beliefs of the Jehovah's Witnesses, so we had this bond that others didn't completely understand. Eventually we started having sex before marriage, which was not allowed. After a few weeks, Trout decided to go tell the brothers about our intimacy. In the end I was what they call "disfellowshipped" (basically disowned and shunned from my family and congregation), but he was not! Since he had come forward and told, the brothers felt that he was repentant but that I wasn't. In truth I wasn't sorry. I loved him, and I had chosen him over the organization, but he didn't choose me.

My dad gave me three weeks to move out. For a while I was homeless and got myself into some pretty bad situations trying to survive. I had been raised in a bubble and was very naive. I had to grow up fast. I think my parents thought this would make me come running back and be sorry, but it did the opposite. It hurt me so badly that I didn't want anything to do with the organization ever again. I loved my family and was devastated, but I was exhausted and done. I didn't stop believing most of the thoughts I had been taught, but what I did know was that it didn't resonate with me. I was so hurt that even if I died at Armageddon, like I had been taught, I would rather die than serve a God that ripped families apart. At least those were my thoughts at the time.

I was in the wind. Life was wagging me like a dog's tail. I was just responding and trying to survive. I was not actively creating my life, just doing whatever was in front of me. When I stopped being a Witness, I believed I was a sinner who would die at Armageddon, but I just couldn't do what I needed to do. I had begun to question what I had been taught but was also afraid to question what I was taught. I went through years of pain in a conflicted, stuck state. During these years I do not remember getting many intuitive hits. I was completely in my story and was just trying to survive life.

During this time I had an amazing son. Even though there were beliefs that did not sit right with me out of fear, I still had my parents take my son to the meetings. I could be a sinner, but I didn't want Jehovah to take it out on my son. I wanted him saved. The truth is, my son saved my life because he gave me a purpose and a reason to do whatever it took to create a home, job, and stable life for us.

I remember that one time, my parents had a huge anniversary party, and my brother called and asked if I would bring my son, but I was not invited. I wanted to be a part of my family, and it was devastatingly painful. I went several years not doing anything to break their rules such as having sex before marriage, celebrating the holidays, drinking, or doing drugs; basically I was living like a Jehovah's Witness but not going to the meetings.

Then my mom had a stroke in 2006, and suddenly, as I was the only girl, my family needed me. I was so grateful to be able to spend time with my mom, nursing her. I missed her so much. Her recovery was slow. After three months she was finally able to come home. One night I took dinner over, and my dad thanked me for the food, but then he said, "You know you can't stay here for dinner." He couldn't see me as a person because of his beliefs. So I went home and thought about it for a few days, and I decided to have a talk with him.

He was in a shed in the backyard behind his house. It was a big deal to confront my dad. It is something I didn't do. I said to him, "I don't understand why you can't look at me and know I'm a good person. Why do you need the brothers in the congregation to tell you? I have done nothing to break your rules. I work and take care of my son. Why can't you look at me and know I am a good person?"

He looked me in the eyes and said, "April, you are not a good person. I am not proud of you." There was more after that, but I didn't hear the words over the pain going through my heart. I felt like I couldn't breathe.

That was a big turning point. It created such a wedge—it was such an unloving act. He was angry and punishing me because I wasn't doing or being what he wanted me to be.

I now realize that he was so scared. Scared to lose control. Scared to be wrong because then his whole life would have been built on lies. So scared to just love me over his thoughts because that would have destroyed his world. It was time. Because of the pain, I didn't want anything to do with them. All of these things happening together rattled my story even more.

ALONG CAME DENNIS

The year was 2003. I was twenty-eight at this point, and my son was eight. This is the year I also met an amazing man named Dennis. The separation from my family and the love of this amazing man in my life allowed me to start stepping into who I was as a person. Dennis loved and accepted me. This allowed me to start to heal and really be me. I would have nightmares that I was running from Armageddon. It was chasing me, and I was trying to save my son from it.

Dennis played an instrumental part in helping me listen to my intuitive hits versus ignoring or discrediting them. At this time in my life, I didn't know how to not take on other people's emotions. If someone nearby me was experiencing an extreme emotion (anger, rage, or mourning), it would overwhelm me. One time Dennis and I were walking in the produce section at a grocery store; I was hit by the frequency of mourning. My heart came up into my throat, and I was overwhelmed with grief.

Dennis turned around and looked at me. "What's wrong?"

With a cracking voice, I said, "She's mourning!" I was trying to motion at a woman without pointing.

He looked at me with this puzzled expression and looked over at a woman five feet away pushing a cart with a child in it. "What are you taking about?" he asked me.

Now, I was reading him also, and I could tell he was confused. The sensations started to get better as she moved forward and we moved away. I asked, "Can't you feel that? She's mourning!"

He looked at her and then at me, and again at her. He said, "I can see she's sad by the look on her face, but why do you think she's mourning?"

Reading him, I could see that he was baffled. In shock, I said very loudly, "*Really?* You can't feel that? Everyone in the store should be able to feel that!"

That was the first time I realized not everyone feels at the same intensity. It is similar to a sense of smell; some people can smell every little thing, and others aren't able to smell much at all.

Dennis was not scared of what I felt or saw. He never judged me or made me feel like I was bad or crazy. He gave me this beautiful platform where I could experience my intuition without holding back. From there, it was on! "Did you feel that? Did you hear that? Did you see that?" Most of the time he answered no, but every once in a while, if the sensation was really strong, he would be like, "Oh, yes, I felt that!"

This was also the start of my acceptance that I was not just talking to imaginary friends but I was indeed connecting to the essences of people no longer in the form. Dennis's stepfather had passed away prior to our meeting, but when he would talk about him, I could feel him and describe how he was as a person, and he would join in the conversation with us. His stepfather was not a man of many words. He had a dry since of humor, but when he did talk, it was straight to the point. I could feel him more than he talked to me, but this was the type of person he was, according to people who knew him. This was not easy for me to accept, and I honestly didn't like doing it. It scared me. I didn't know how to explain it or what I was even doing for sure. Regardless, it kept happening and growing.

I had been taught so many beliefs that were standing in the way of me being able to see, hear, and feel my intuition, but all of that was about to change.

CHAPTER 2

Stripped of My Story

⚜

THE NEXT BIG EVENT WAS in October 2007. I was petrified to go to the dentist. They lightly sedated me, and I had an experience while I was there. It was as if someone took my hand and walked me back through my life. This happened within a couple of minutes. I was shown that every decision I had made was controlled by the thoughts I had been taught and believed. I didn't know how to not function from the script. All I knew was what I had been taught. I was never taught to go within and ask what is right or wrong for me. I was *told* what was right for me and who I was supposed to be. But what about *my* truth? What about what is deep inside me? That's what I woke up to that day in the dentist office. What if everything I had been taught was just thoughts? If I didn't believe those thoughts, would I have lived my life differently? Would I be different? Would I feel different?

I was in shock for twenty-four to forty-eight hours afterward. I couldn't come out of that deep inner reflective place. Dennis and I were sitting in the car when, finally, the pain just started pouring out of me. I tried to put into words what I had seen. It felt like in that moment, my whole story was ripped away from me. Who I was as a *being*, without the story, was being shown to me. That was the first time I had a glimpse of freedom from my story.

It's truly hard to explain what it's like to feel free but devastated. It was amazing to be free from my childhood beliefs because, for one, that meant I wasn't going to die at Armageddon. It also meant I had lost my family and community *over thoughts*. The heartache and devastation that believing thoughts had created was heart wrenching for me. At first I tried to run around and tell my family the thoughts were not true, but that created a lot of problems. I soon realized that when you believe a story as your truth, it is very hard to let go and wake up.

There is a weird safety in having a story about life. If that story isn't true, then what story is true? I started to research all kinds of worldly religions. I felt so unearthed during this time. What you believe creates who you believe you are as a person. It didn't occur to me that no story is needed to just be. Animals do it all the time, but humans panic and believe that a story is needed to exist. *A story is needed for the ego to exist but not for a being to exist.* In time I came to realize this, but I had not yet. I was frantic to find an identity. I was unable to believe any new thoughts, like I had the thoughts taught to me as a child. As a child, I had no resistance or questioning. If my parents said it was true, I believed it, and this became my truth. By believing the thoughts, it made it true for me. As I studied other thoughts, they were now just that—thoughts! Some resonated more with me or were interesting, but I couldn't fall under their illusion as my identity.

This was the beginning of my understanding that the *only* thing that gives a thought power is a person believing it. The word "believe" is so powerful. Prior to believing a thought, it is nothing. Once a thought is believed, it then creates emotions and opinions.

Believing thoughts also creates something far more serious, which is time. The actual act of believing a thought happens in the now, but what the thought is *about* always creates time. Even if your thought was about the moment, the moment had to have happened in order for you to label it or think about it. The *act* of thinking is in the now, but what the thoughts are *about* creates the illusion of time.

For example, if you believe the thought "Life is hard," it will create emotions within you and many opinions. You will go into the illusion (a story in your head) of time and give examples or proof to support this thought. Your body will go through all the emotions—anger, frustration, irritation, disappointment, and unfairness—that go along with the thought "Life is hard." You could be sitting in a beautiful, peaceful garden and still go through all these emotions. Every thought believed is like this.

There are thoughts constantly floating through the mind. Just because you think a thought does not mean you believe it. *The acts of thinking and believing are two different things.* If someone said to you, "That person is a horrible person" and you do not believe that thought, it will travel through and out of your mind. If you do believe it, then emotions about that person and examples of why you feel that way will follow.

Eventually this led me to not pay attention to whether a thought was true or false, good or bad, because I knew the only thing that made a thought true or false was a person believing it. I started to pay attention to the effects created by believing different thoughts. For example, what emotions did it invoke in the person? What behaviors? Where did they go in time? How was it affecting their relationships? How was it affecting their lives? How was it affecting their health?

This is so important that I'm going to say it again: the *only* thing that makes a thought true or false is a person believing it as so. So many undesirable things are experienced over and over again because the mind replays stories it believes that never happen in reality, or only happen once.

Because of this, I spent the next several years letting go of thoughts (stories). This did not happen overnight. As I went through different situations in life, it would dawn on me what I believed as truth and needed to let go of. For example, because I believed I was going to die at Armageddon, I had always held myself emotionally away from my son. I believed that I was going to die, and I would have to give him up so he could live. When I realized that was not true, it was horribly painful to realize that all those years, I had held myself back from him instead of just allowing him to be close to me. Believing these thoughts did years of damage, which did not heal or become undone overnight.

Without me realizing it, *my intuition was getting stronger as my story was dissipating.* My intuition had *always* been a part of me; I was just distracted by the stories (thoughts) over hearing or feeling the intuitive senses.

Around this time, people started to look like spiderwebs to me, fragmented all throughout time, past and future. I came to realize that *believing* stories and being lost in thoughts created this.

SPLIT BETWEEN TWO WORLDS

I was starting to be recognized as a person who could read other people and talk to the other side within my circle of friends. A friend said to me one time, "Why do you always see the negative in people when reading them?" This question hurt me. I went through so much judgment and criticism growing up that I tried very hard not to judge or be critical of people. But I couldn't control what I intuitively sensed. This comment eventually helped me unlock something very big, which I share later in this book.

Never in a million years did I think I would do this for a living or at the level at which I am now doing it. I was still very uncomfortable with my intuition, although I was fascinated with it. I was very focused on making it in the world as a real estate developer. As the CFO for a large developer, I was well on my way to accomplishing that dream. I had become hard and emotionally detached from life and people. My drive to be enough and to be successful controlled my life. I now realize that my intuitive abilities helped me greatly in the corporate world to read people, situations, and outcomes. It was such a part of me, I didn't even realize I was doing it.

It was around this time that I was introduced to smoking weed. I took to it right away because for the first time ever, it helped me shut down and not be so driven or hard on myself. I had no idea how to just let go, accept life, or be happy. It was also unhealthy because shutting off my pain and not hearing myself enabled me to work even harder and dishonor myself even more emotionally to accomplish my unhealthy expectations. So much of my story I had let go of, but the deeper human programming was still there.

During this time, out of the blue, I would become aware of stories I still had within me. This was very challenging at times. "Aha moments" do not always come at appropriate times. I remember one time sitting at my desk talking with an important client. All of a sudden, I got an intuitive hit that she lived in a state of being in trouble with her own self. Her parents taught her this because they were also tied into this story, so it was impossible for them not to teach it to her. Of course she didn't realize she believed she was in trouble all of the time or what she put her body through out of fear of being in trouble. As this was happening, what I was actually more aware of was that I too had invested energetically in this story. I unconsciously believed and acted like I was in trouble *all* of the time. This created me being in trouble constantly within myself, so it was impossible for me not to create this around me in the outside world. When this realization hit me on the phone with her, with all the years of emotional stress I had put myself through over an untrue pattern (belief), I was so devastated that I almost couldn't tell her I had to get off the phone, my voice was cracking so badly. I stood up and headed toward the women's bathroom because I knew there was no stopping what was about to come out of me. I went in one of the bathroom stalls and sobbed for at least an hour. I could see that throughout my whole life, I had been in trouble with myself, and when I was in trouble with myself, I punished myself. Although these releases were healing and freeing, our society is not set up to allow this kind of healing and evolving. I did my best to maneuver through a very hard time in my life while still trying to maintain way too much in my life.

INNER COMPASS

Although I was going through a lot in life, as everyone does, my intuition was getting stronger, and I was constantly figuring out new things I could read or do with it. One time, Dennis and I decided to find a friend's house we had never been to by only using my intuition. We knew in what suburb in San Diego, California, they lived, but that was it. I had always been really good at direction and finding my way around, but I just thought I inherited that from my dad, who was also amazing at directions.

I started by telling Dennis, "Well it feels like they live over at the end of Magnolia where the road turns to dirt." So we headed over there. The entire way, it felt right in my body, like we were heading in the right direction. Once we got to the dirt road about halfway down, it suddenly felt like we had gone too far.

I told Dennis, "We need to go back." So he turned around and slowed down.

I told him, "It feels like we need to turn left, like they live over there somewhere." So he turned left and drove down an even smaller dirt road. There was a house on a little bit of a hill, and I said, "It feels like that one. I can even see our friend possibly smoking and throwing his cigarette butts down that hill."

Sure enough, Dennis walked to the bottom of the hill, and there were cigarette butts. No one was home at the time, so eventually we looked in the mailbox—and lo and behold, the name on the mail was our friend's. There were many times that Dennis and I went on adventures to develop and explore my intuition.

NEW PATHS APPEAR

Even with all of the intuitive growth, I still felt very lost, like I was hurting and killing myself trying to be enough. Of course, I crashed and burned. I shut down emotionally for about six months. Thank goodness Dennis was there to take care of my son and me. During this time, a friend gave me a book by Carolyn Myss. For those of you who are not familiar with her work, she used to be one of the strongest medical intuitives in the world. I say "used to be" because she no longer does readings; she mainly teaches. Finally I found someone who had put into words what I was seeing and feeling. This book opened me up to a whole new world of thoughts. What would it be like to develop my intuition as a medical intuitive and do it as a career? The idea was enticing to me. Once that thought came into my awareness, I started to attract new learning opportunities into my world. Up until this point, I had been very fascinated with how thought patterns affected people. Carolyn Myss's work helped me take that to the next level. I started to profile in people how thought patterns were affecting their cell tissue and health. This was something I could always do, but I was not aware of it. Awareness opened up the door for me to start looking at it and understanding it. I did not receive a treasure box marked Medical Intuitive Hits. I just needed to start paying attention to what I was seeing, hearing, and feeling to develop.

I had never tried to see cell tissue or feel it. This was new and exciting but frustrating because I didn't understand everything I was seeing or feeling. For example, when I sense high blood pressure, I see an impression of the circulatory system pulsating really hard with the rhythm of the heart. In the beginning I had no idea what that meant. Eventually I figured out it meant high blood pressure. Everything about medical intuition was like that. I don't intuitively hear or see the medical term "cancer." I see the actual cell tissue and describe it. But again, I didn't know that meant cancer until

I slowly matched up what I was seeing and feeling to what Western medical doctors label it.

HAWAII ADVENTURE

About this time in my life, Dennis decided he wanted to pursue obtaining his diving instructor certificate. That required one thousand hours in the water. In San Diego, the ocean water is very dark and cold. So we decided to move to Maui, Hawaii, in June of 2008. I'm sharing this part of my life because it was the first time I almost completely functioned from my intuitive hits. We decided to sell *everything* we owned; we only kept nine suitcases of stuff. We had no storage at all and sold everything in three weeks. (I think because we did it so fast, we didn't have much time to mourn selling everything until after the fact.) Without our knowing it, this also helped us release years of history.

One strange thing that started to happen during the process of moving was that every day, I would get really scared and tell Dennis, "I keep feeling and seeing an earthquake." It would get so bad, I would make him take me out of the house to calm my nervous system. Dennis believed me because he had witnessed my intuition being right so many times. Finally, after about four days of this, while we were out, Dennis noticed the front page of a newspaper that showed the catastrophic 2008 earthquake in China. Because we had been packing and moving, we had not watched the news or had any idea of this huge event. But I could feel it because so many lives had been affected, and it created a huge energy wave through the earth and humans.

Since we moved in only three weeks, I ended up booking our plane tickets prior to figuring out how to ship our car. My intuition told me to book our fight on June 3. Dennis was concerned about this, but my sensation was so strong, I did it anyway. We had to turn over the keys to our home on May 31, which meant we would need to stay in a hotel for a few nights. We had no idea how to ship our car. On one of our forced drives, because I was freaking out about the earthquake, we decided to drive downtown and see if we could find where cars are shipped to Hawaii. We lived about thirty-five minutes from downtown San Diego. I'm laughing as I think about the craziness of this story, but we had time to burn, and why not? Once we got close to downtown, I started my usual "it feels like" dialogue: "It feels left—no, it feels like we went too far; it feels like you need to go further..." and so on. Finally, we drove up to a gated fence and decided to just ask the guys at the gate if they knew where cars were shipped to Hawaii. The guy said, "Here. Well, you drop it off here, but you have to go online to book it first!" Yes, we had indeed found the exact place to ship cars! (Downtown San Diego is not small, but we found it.)

Then, we went home and discovered online that cars are only shipped once a month, and it takes a week to ship. The shipping date was May 28, arriving in Maui on June 4. Now, remember, I had booked our plane tickets to arrive in Oahu, Hawaii, on June 3. Come to find out, our plane was going to land too late on the third to take the ferry over to Maui. We had to stay one night in Oahu and take the ferry on the fourth in the morning. Once on Maui, we could then take a taxi to pick up our car, which would just have arrived.

Over and over again, my intuition proved to be right on as we went through this very fast move. Something I learned from going through this is that so many people have a belief that intuition is not practical. But it's just the opposite. Intuition is so in the moment, step by step, that people get bored or just don't listen to it. Intuition is not just some big dream in the future of what you could become. Intuition is simple: do this, now do this, now do this, and so on. But first you have to listen, and then be brave enough to act and trust.

I honestly did not do very well in Hawaii. It's very different to go there and stay in a big hotel versus actually moving there, renting a place, and trying to survive. My son loved it and fit in extremely well with the local kids. We rented a place right next to a YMCA, and he was over there all the time. Since I had been off work for the six months prior to the move, I wasn't ready to reenter full-time accounting or consulting work. I got a job at a coffee shop that I truly enjoyed. I had never had a simple job with minimal responsibilities. After six months, I realized that for many reasons, we could not stay there. It was expensive; I was worried about my son's education, and in order for me to pursue developing my intuition in the medical field, I needed to find a doctor to work with. I moved back to San Diego, leaving my son and Dennis in Hawaii. I stayed with friends, got a job in three weeks, and started to save money for a place to live. Dennis and my son joined me in San Diego after a month. We rented a place in North San Diego because the school district at that time was the best. We started to rebuild our lives in San Diego again.

I also met a doctor within *three* weeks of moving back to San Diego!

CHAPTER 3

Dr. Karen

❖

WHEN MOVING BACK TO CALIFORNIA, one of my main goals was to find a doctor with whom I could work. Within three weeks of moving back, I met Dr. Karen Van Hoesen!

A reverend friend (we will call her Susan) invited me to attend her Sunday morning service. I felt a need to go, although I didn't know why. During the service, I noticed a woman in the group with beautiful bright-red hair who had wonderful energy. Curiosity bubbled out of her. After the service was over, I immediately approached her, and we engaged in a general conversation, getting to know one another.

About this time, Reverend Susan walked up and said, "I'm so glad the two of you met. I was going to introduce you. This is Dr. Karen Van Hoesen and—"

As soon as Reverend Susan said Karen was a doctor, I interrupted her and said, "Do you know who Carolyn Myss is?" I knew if Karen was aware of Carolyn Myss's work, she would know what a medical intuitive was.

Karen said, "Yes, I love her work!"

I said, "I'm a medical intuitive!"

Karen said, "Want to come into the emergency department with me?"

Yes, it happened that fast—too fast for me to process, because I actually felt scared inside. So I asked her, "Can we go get coffee first?" I laugh as I tell this wonderful story. Meeting Karen so fast was not only surprising, but it was also the beginning of an amazing adventure and friendship.

We met for coffee two days later, and eight days after that, I went into the ED for the first time. I was scared to death. Scared of failing. Scared of not meeting Karen's expectations, whatever those were. Scared of not being able to read fast enough. Scared of being wrong. Scared I wouldn't get any intuitive hits at all because of my fear. But I was there with a deep knowing inside: this was important and was the start of something bigger.

I will never forget it as long as I live. Karen standing at the doc box door saying to me, "The patient would be dead already!" This was because I read so slowly back then. The comment hurt me but was true and pushed me to learn faster ways to read people, which I did! I can't remember how I discovered this, but it occurred to me that if I looked at the body as a target practice and intuitively asked, "Where is the largest energy loss?" I would then see this red smog coming out of the body. This was the largest energy loss. Then I could go to that area and focus on it more closely. The largest energy loss was not always the reason the patient had come into the ED. This was/is very important!

Karen's version of meeting me follows:

"When I met April, I was familiar with medical intuition through books I had read, but I had no practical experience working with an intuit. I wanted to understand what April was able to read and how accurate she was. From the very first day, I was amazed at not only how well April could read a patient's physical symptoms, but that she could tell me the underlying thought patterns that caused those symptoms. She was definitely slow in the beginning, but with time, her speed at reading a patient's energy and her accuracy greatly improved."

READING FROM THE DOC BOX

When I first started to go into the ED with Karen, I did not go into the patients' rooms. Instead, I would stay in the doc box, and Karen would come in with a patient's first name and age for me to read. One day, within the first month of research, Karen had me read an older man. As soon as I stepped into his energy, my chest was tight, I couldn't breathe, my heart was aching, and my left arm hurt. As I experienced this, I spoke out loud to Karen.

She looked at me, puzzled. She was quiet for a minute and then asked, "Okay, can you go lower and tell me what you see?"

So I pushed the sensations of his heart away and looked lower. I then noticed a dark-black hole in my foot. My foot and lower leg hurt. I was wearing a dress that day and picked up a pen off the counter. My left leg was crossed over my right leg. On my left leg, I started to draw lines up my leg from my foot toward my knee. I finally looked up at Karen; she had a blank look on her face that was very hard for me to read. Then, without saying anything, she got up and walked out. (Yes, I was sitting and drawing on myself in front of a world-renowned doctor just so you can understand the complete picture!) I sat there, not sure if the research program was over because she thought I was crazy or if something I had said to her had struck a chord.

Finally, after about forty-five minutes, she came back in the doc box. (Longest forty-five minutes ever!) She sat down and said, "About three weeks ago, this man came into the ED. He had stepped on a nail, and we treated him with a tetanus shot and antibiotic. He went home and stopped taking his antibiotic. The infection worsened and is now spreading up his leg. The lines you were drawing are almost identical to the red lines of his infection. But when you said what you did about his heart, it made me wonder, and I went back in and asked him if he was having shortness of breath or chest pain. He answered yes but didn't say anything because he was so worried about his leg. After getting an EKG, it was confirmed that his heart was in distress from his overwhelming infection, and he was also having a heart attack."

Wow! At this point, I really needed the validation. It helped me trust what I had been seeing and started to build a relationship between Karen and myself. As Karen started to see and understand how I read people, her biggest fascination was not with what was wrong with them medically but with the underlying "why" that led to the medical condition in the first place.

SPEED, ACCURACY, AND UNDERSTANDING INCREASING

I had been in the ED about a year when a man came in with chest pain. As I read his heart, I could see that it was closed off. It was confirmed by an EKG and blood work that he had a blockage in one of his arteries supplying his heart and was having a myocardial infarction (heart attack). As I read the thoughts and emotions within his heart, I could see that he had blocked love from flowing through his heart. I could see a daughter that he had written out of his life, an ex-wife that he hated, and family that he disassociated from. His own self-love was nonexistent. His heart felt very cold and shut down to me. As I looked deeper at why he had done this, it was because of fear. He had a very strong fear of getting hurt. It was easier to just push people away or cut them off. He used being right and passing judgment to give himself reasons to cut people off and not love them. His physical cell tissue then mirrored his thought process and blocked love within the bloodlines (the circulatory system mirrors family bloodlines).

Karen recalls another case:

"I remember one patient that the paramedics brought in who was acting very erratic and confused; he almost tipped the gurney over because he was thrashing around and had to be sedated. April told me that she felt a lot of pressure on the right side of his brain and that she saw blood on the brain. Sure enough, the CT scan of his head showed bleeding on the top of the brain, which was causing his symptoms."

ENERGETIC DNA

One time, while Karen and I were sitting in the doc box reviewing patients, she asked me if there was always a story (thoughts) behind a physical ailment. Was it possible to just have bad luck? Was it always the person's fault? What about young children? I looked at her and said, "It is *impossible* for there to be a physical ailment without a story and emotions. I always find a story within the body supporting whatever is happening physically. It would be like a building floating in midair with no structure to support the building."

Physical DNA is created in part by what I have termed cognitive DNA and emotional DNA. The thoughts a person believes to be true (conscious or unconscious) creates cognitive DNA and plays a role in determining physical matter. How a person processes emotions and his or her relationship with emotions creates emotional DNA and plays a role in determining physical matter as well.

This means that a mother and father are not just passing on physical traits. They are passing on their family history, emotions, and how they process emotions. These things create an energetic blueprint for physical DNA. This is not about blame. It's no one's so-called fault. We live in a world of cause and effect. No one deserves to be sick. It's not about deserving.

Would you expect a cookie cutter to cut a different shape cookie than it is shaped? In order to change the shape of the cookie, you would have to change the cookie cutter. You would never say to the cookie cutter, "You're bad! Look at the shape you created!" It does what it does. A human being's physical DNA blueprint (cookie cutter) is energetic, not physical, which means that, as you let go of thoughts believed (cognitive DNA) and change your relationship with emotions (emotional DNA), your physical DNA changes.

No Time for the "Why"

Karen was always more interested in the "why." Why are they sick? What thoughts and emotions are supporting the physical ailment being treated? But sometimes, due to the severity of the patient, there was no time for the why. In these situations I was only reading the cell tissue as fast as I could. One day as I arrived, Karen met me in a rush. As we walked rapidly through the ED to a patient's room, she gave me his first name and age. I quickly said I see a hot iron burning a hole through his stomach and his life force pouring out of the hole. My stomach was burning and killing me. I was clutching my stomach as I said this to her. She immediately entered the room where there was an unconscious man and several other doctors and nurses working on him. I stood back, listened, and watched.

Prior to me arriving, this patient had come to the ED with partial paralysis, low blood pressure, and low heart rate; he was unconscious. Later, Karen told me her initial thoughts were that he was suffering from a stroke or heart attack. When I told her what I had seen and felt, it occurred to her that maybe he had an ulcer that was bleeding internally that was causing his symptoms. His blood work came back, and his hemoglobin was extremely low, confirming that he was bleeding internally and needed surgery. In surgery, they discovered a bleeding ulcer.

Karen and I were making huge breakthroughs in energy medicine, but as she explains here, due to the environment of the ED and current limiting beliefs of Western medicine, we were not sure how to move our research forward:

"I was still learning to listen to and trust April's impressions because she often pointed me in a direction that wasn't initially obvious with my own history and physical exam but ended up being extremely important in the overall diagnosis and care of the patient. I was becoming more fascinated with the energy and thoughts behind what created disease in the body in the first place. Even if April was able to see and feel those thoughts within the cell tissue, I had no idea how to use that information to help a patient heal."

As my confidence grew and more people started to recognize me as an intuit, I decided to start teaching what I termed "energy education." This step increased my intuition. It's one thing to know it within your mind, but once I had to start putting it into language, it became more real for me.

I set up a little office with a good-sized conference room where I was able to teach and see clients. I started to see clients, but my favorite thing was holding energy education classes. Not only was I learning from the ED, but I was now also learning from clients and groups.

CHAPTER 4

Energy Education

⚜

I'VE ALWAYS SAID THE GREATEST benefit I receive when I do a reading is that I learn as I teach. What I read in people is not knowledge that April Dawn Corbitt has. So as I intuitively see, hear, and feel new things, I have aha moments within me. At some level, to a greater or lesser degree, I need to let go of the same beliefs I find in people I'm reading. *I (you) let go when you stop believing thought as truth.*

People were now coming to me to learn how to develop intuition. It was not easy putting into words what I saw or experienced in a teachable way. This is not something that can be obtained from an outside source. You cannot say to someone, "Feel this for me!" It is an experience you have to sense. I was trying to explain what that experience felt like and how to break down any blocks that stood in the way of sensing. If intuition is already a part of you, then why are you not feeling it, listening to it, and honoring it? That is how I approached teaching intuition.

Because this material will not soak in after only hearing it once, I teach this material in different ways and with different formats. You will absorb it today, and then you will have aha moments that help you understand the material deeper and deeper over time.

Not realizing it, I was teaching about energy more than I was teaching people how to access their intuition. Eventually I come to understand the difference, but not at that point in time.

Developing Your Intuition 101

First, you must be clear to sense your senses! Clear of what? Clear of time and in the present moment. What creates time is attachment to thoughts. (I explain this in greater detail under the section about time.) This also means being clear of substances that numb or alter your senses. Intuition is not a trip in the mind induced by some drug. Remember, I smoked weed for many years. There was a time I thought weed helped me read more clearly, but now that I am clear, I can tell you with certainty that this is not true. My readings are much more accurate and precise without any substances. Your emotions also need to be clear. You cannot feel your senses if your body is overwhelmed, angry, frustrated, and so on. I'm not saying emotions are bad. When your body is clear of emotions, you can read another person's emotions without confusing them with yours.

Second, you have to want to connect. Connecting is not something that just happens when you're clear. It is an actual step. I can be completely clear and peaceful but not connected to the plants, earth, or the person in front of me. Connecting with people, places, and things through your senses is different than connecting through your thoughts. Your thoughts can put into words what someone feels, but you have to feel them first. I do not walk around being connected to everything and everyone. I have always found it funny when people get nervous to be around me because they are scared I'm going to read their thoughts or know their secrets. I laugh and say, "I spend hours trying to get out of my own thoughts; trust me, I don't want to hear yours!"

Third, trusting your intuition is crucial but can be hard in the beginning because you want validation. Start with this: I'm confident that I am an intuitive *being*. I'm confident I feel things, hear things, get impressions, and know things that are beyond my mind knowledge. I do not always understand what I sense, but I am confident that I do sense them. I am not crazy or different. I am confident that if I listen to my intuition, it will start to grow, make more sense, and get stronger.

Fourth, there are no words to describe the courage it takes to honor your intuition. Courage is important if you want your intuition to grow. It takes a huge amount of courage to listen to your intuition. Think about this. If you cannot or will not act on small intuitive hits, then what good would it do you to get a bigger, more profound intuitive hit? Intuition is moment by moment: go do this, now go do that, and so on. It's not bossy or going to parent or punish you. It's a sense. You have a choice to listen to it. What I can tell you is your senses always have your best interest at heart. I cannot say that about the thoughts floating around in your head. Your thoughts could be that, you are not enough, you are fat, or you always do it wrong. Your senses will tell you that if you eat that you will get sick or feel too full, or this situation is not right for you. There are millions of reasons we do not honor our intuition. "Reasons" are always thoughts believed! Possibly you might believe that mind knowledge is more important than intuition. Maybe you are petrified of being embarrassed, being wrong, or failing, or maybe you just don't like the intuitive answer you're getting, so you don't want to listen. This is why courage is essential to develop your intuition.

TIME

Time is intuition's largest block. Intuition is a sense. Senses only happen in the moment. People are fragmented throughout the past by holding on to it, and people are fragmented into the future because they are constantly projecting themselves there. You can *only* feel your intuition in the space of *now*, not in a future moment or past moment, which means the fragmentation makes it impossible to feel your senses.

Although intuitive hits are far more important and useful than any thought, we live in a world that does not understand this yet. Every human *being* is waking up from the illusion of time. People are different when it comes to where they are fragmented or project themselves, and it changes moment by moment. Someone might be 69 percent in the past, 28 percent in the future, leaving only about 3 percent in the moment to create his or her life or feel intuition. A different person could be 90 percent in the future, 9 percent in the past, leaving only 1 percent in the now. This also changes moment by moment, depending on what people are thinking about. The last example I gave would change greatly if that person's father had just passed away or the person received a call from his or her mom discussing family and history. What doesn't change is that currently as a species, we are constantly engaging in leaving the now.

Why is this, you might ask? In short, it is because we are all scared to live. In the now is the only place you can create life, and if we are never in the now, then we do not have to live. What are we scared of? We're scared of embarrassment, failure, criticism, surviving, hurting, rejection, what others might think or say, loss, change, the unknown, emotions, obligation, accountability, responsibility, safety, and thousands of other things. We're scared of being wrong, not being enough, living being hard, being out of control, not being loved or never being loved again, being judged, being uncomfortable, being alone, getting in trouble, not meeting expectations, being vulnerable, not being smart enough, losing freedom, things not working out, letting people down, and making the wrong decision.

I believe people are more scared to live then die.

We are each very powerful when completely present and moving with our intuition. If we are present in each moment, creating at 100 percent, we would create things very quickly. At first you might think you want to create things in your life quickly, but upon deeper pondering, you might find that you are afraid of what it would take to create things instantly.

The rate at which we create or do not create depends on how many fearful blocks you have to move through. I cannot tell you how many times I've done readings and told people they had options in their energy field to create whatever (new job, relationship, house, friends) if they went after it, and they respond with something like, "Oh, no, not now." This is backed up with lots of reasons why they can't move.

Part of developing your intuition is being brave enough to live, being okay with being a powerful creator of your life. When you get an intuitive hit to move or act, you do! Why get an intuitive hit to create something huge and amazing when you struggle in the now with small intuitive hits? It all starts in the now, *not in time*, with small intuitive hits, which builds up to something huge.

LAYERING

Thoughts and emotions are like peeling an onion. I'm sure you have heard this before. It describes well how one thought or emotion supports another and then another.

I used to write this example on the board to illustrate layering and how it works.

Fear = Control = Power = Some tool of power

When most people experience fear, they deal with it by trying to control. If they can control a situation, person, or outcome, it gives them a false sense of safety. In order to have control, you must have power. At this point, it can branch off into many different things, depending on the relationship and situation. Trying to make someone feel guilty is a tool of power. The thoughts "I know more" or "I am right" are tools of power. Authority or position (parent, rank, age) are tools of power. One believed thought leads to another thought and then another and another, which creates layering. This is why when I'm reading someone, I ask, "Why?" many times.

For example, I will see a person who needs to be right. I will intuitively ask why. I will then see that the person is using it as a false sense of power because he or she is trying to control a person's choices. Okay, why? I will see it is because the person is scared of losing this other person. Through asking why, I discovered layering and how truly complex human behavior and motives are. Most human behavior is unconscious.

Let us back into this, like I would read it. A friend is saying to me, "I don't know! I just don't know!" I ask, "Why does she not know?" It feels like she does know but doesn't like the answer she is getting about her boyfriend. I ask, "Why doesn't she like the answer?" I see that if he truly is this way, then she would be faced with making a decision. I ask, "Why doesn't she want to make a decision?" I see that if she faced reality, she could not, within herself, condone living in the situation anymore. I ask, "Why doesn't she want to move or save herself from this situation if she knows it's not right for her?" I get that it is because she is scared. Having a little love is better than being alone is her thoughts. So she uses not knowing to not move. This example is not good or bad, but it demonstrates layering and how asking "Why?" when reading situations can help reveal the layering.

Here is a second example, using the same sentence but different layering. A client says to me that she "doesn't know what to do." I ask, "Why does she not know what to do?" I see that she is trying to figure out something in the future, and not all factors to make this decision are yet known. I ask, "Then why is she trying to figure it out before she needs to or can?" I see that she projects herself a lot into the future versus living now. I ask, "Why is she doing this?" I see that worrying about a future moment means she does not have to focus on now. It's a distraction. I ask, "Why does she not want to focus on the now?" I see that she doesn't want to do anything in the now. "Why?" I see that she really doesn't want to live for a lot of reasons. She could get up and go find a hobby, but then her excuse would be something like, "There really isn't anything to do in this little town." She could get up and write, but then she would say, "I'm not in the mood." She could get up and find a group to support her, but then again, she would have to move. She does not want to move. There is a false safety in being stuck and doing nothing. So she keeps her mind busy with things that she does not need to figure out yet or can't figure out yet.

Every reading is different. Every why is different! I find it interesting when people say, "Oh, read me, read me!" They're all excited, as if it's that easy to do. It's not that reading people is hard, but trying to map a person's programming is extremely complicated and involved. It is not something you can do in a few sentences or even hours.

RELATIONSHIPS WITH ENERGIES

As I stated earlier, I do not look at different energies as good or bad. I look at the effects they are having on your experiences of life, relationships, and cell tissue. Any energy that is blocked, suppressed, or rejected can create undesirable things in life. Even love blocked, suppressed, or rejected will create issues within the heart. Our bodies are designed to flow, not to hold on to or stop the flow. Think about this! Is there any part of your body that does not flow—your circulatory system, your digestive tract? In fact, if your circulatory system or digestive tract stopped flowing, you would not be able to live. Nothing about our bodies tells us that it is healthy for us to block, suppress, or cut off the flow of emotions or the flow of thoughts. So by looking at your relationship with all energies, you will change your health and experience of life.

Building a relationship with all energies will also increase your intuition. If you have a horrible relationship with anger, you will not be objective to read it in yourself or someone else.

Energies are like piano chords to me. One is not better than another but can get out of tune (proportion) if the flow is blocked or obstructed. All chords have their places. All energies have their places, even anger. If you kick my dog, I'm going to get angry and protect him. If you're angry only about the situation in the moment, it is manageable and reasonable. Anger becomes overwhelming and unreasonable when it has built up for years. I'm sure you have engaged with someone who is upset in this moment versus someone who has years of anger built up that spills into the current conversation. One is digestible, and the other is overwhelming and can seem way over the top.

When we have a good relationship with all energies, we allow them to flow through us in each moment and do not allow years of history to build up within us. When we do this, the different energies are reasonable, manageable, and appropriate.

Energies are neither negative nor positive unless you label them that way and then you experience them that way. They are actually neutral. For example, someone can use anger or rage to kill someone, or they can use that energy as fuel to change laws and protect life. We have witnessed this happen many times when someone's child has been murdered or a drunk driver killed a loved one. Of course he or she is angry, hurt, and full of rage, but the person has decided to let it flow through him or her productively into a cause. It is important how we use the energy. This is *always* based on our relationship with the energy.

I've taught a lot about moving in life, even when you're scared. I have come to realize that hurt debilitates people more than being scared. Everyone's relationship with energies is different. Some people, when scared, become stuck or paralyzed. Some people, when in fear, move even faster. In reading different people's relationships with hurt, I have found that many people want to hide, go to ground, protect themselves, lick their wounds, or feel sorry for themselves. We think we need to heal before we can move. What is your relationship with hurt? How do you act when it is in your body?

When you start to look at your relationship with each energy, you will notice there is a current relationship with the energy that will need to be improved or changed. For example, some people, when they are angry, withdraw because they are afraid of what they will do or say. Some people move into the energy of punishment: "If you make me angry or break my rules, I'm going to punish you!" You will first have to look at what your current relationship is with the energy and then start to slowly work on that relationship, just like you would a marriage or relationship with a child.

BALANCE

When we are learning to master any energy, we experience all spectrums of it. We swing like pendulums. An example of this would be someone's voice that was suppressed when growing up. When the person starts to find his or her voice, in the beginning, the person is very over the top, needing everyone to hear. Eventually, the person finds a balance and learns to hear himself or herself and settle into a middle ground. Another example is work. I'm sure you have heard the saying "work hard, play hard." After a while, these people get exhausted and burned out from the structure needed to work so hard. They do not want to check out just to relax or let go. They find a balance in the middle. They work and do their best to a healthy level so that checking out is not needed. I've also read this in relationships. It is not uncommon if someone has dated a certain personality for many years that when the break up happens, he or she dates people who are completely different. All of these behaviors help us learn different aspects of energies.

I would not label this good or bad. It's like learning to ski and falling over and over again. There is no wrong in the falling, but eventually you can feel your center, and you fall less.

POLAR OPPOSITE

Polar opposite energies neutralize; caring neutralizes neglect, proud neutralizes disappointment, and happiness neutralizes sadness. I've always seen this intuitively as one wave crossing another. The minute a wave going one way makes contact with a wave going the other way, they cross each other out, and the water becomes still. Polar opposite energies do the same. I use to make lists of polar opposites because it helped me neutralize beliefs within people. If someone believed thoughts about being worthless, I knew that thoughts about being important would create balance or neutralize the worthless beliefs. When I encounter some-one who believes he or she is a burden, I tell them the person that he or she is a gift. You can actually feel a person's system calm down when you do this. It's very hard to be hateful to someone who is talking very lovingly to you, or when a person is crying and encounters a person truly laughing from the heart. In fact, if the sad person doesn't want to be happy, he or she will feel irritated or resistant and move away from the laughing in order to not change the mood.

Honor/betrayal
Rage/calm
Pleasure/hurt
Connected/alone
Joy/anger
Scarcity/abundance
Lacking/grateful

This will help you create shifts in your body and moods. It is okay to stay where you are. At times, we just need to feel how we feel until we are ready to let go and feel differently.

THREE FOLDS

There are three folds (aspects) to learning an energy. Let's say the energy is betrayal. You will betray someone, you will be betrayed, and you will betray yourself. This is not good or bad. It's how we learn to play with energies.

If you talk to someone who whittles wood, you will hear about and see the scars on the person's hands. A respect for the knife grows as he or she practices and learns. You will experience the same process with *all* energies. A respect for the energy is acquired as you practice with it in life. As you practice mastering love, hurt, anger, frustration, betrayal, and so on, you will grow to have a deep respect for each energy and how powerful it is. All energies have their place and have thousands of ways for us to use them. *The energy is always neutral. How we use it creates the cause and effect. Intentions and motives give the energies directions.*

I used an example of a cookie cutter earlier in this book. You are the cookie cutter. A simpler term for this is "mold." *What creates the mold is how you are with you.* This is the most powerful contributing factor to how you experience life and what you create in life.

Let's use the energy of abandonment as an example. It is not outside sources that create abandonment in you; it's you holding on to thoughts (stories/histories) about abandonment and you abandoning you. This is very hard at first to swallow because your mind says, "But they left me." If your mind did not tell you they were gone, it would just be another moment. What is actually happening is you are abandoning you by entering time to support the story of abandonment. It takes a very strong person to say, "I'm not going to abandon me in this moment by entertaining thoughts that are not even happening in this moment. I'm going to show up for me and create my life now." Abandoning your life, being lost in the story of abandonment, could create your abandonment of others. While you sit lost in your inner pain, you are not present with others. This is an energy in full swing.

This could also show you how strong your *need* is to hang on to unhappy thoughts. Even if you have resistance to letting go of past stories that make you feel awful, be gentle with yourself as you probe these very sensitive topics. It takes a very brave person to look at his or her relationship with energies: how we use them, how we feel when we use them in different ways, how we act, and what it creates.

I remember once listening to a man share a story about his child's birthday party. He was very upset that ninety people RSVP'd but only about seventy-five showed up. He was explaining how angry he was because they ordered pizza and cake. He was trying to figure out how to accept people's actions. As he talked, the impression I saw was of a man so lost in his disgruntled thoughts that he didn't emotionally show up to the birthday party. His physical body may have been there, but his mind was not.

Another story that comes to mind is of a woman who sat in my classroom very angry and hurt. She said, "I've never been as mean to people as people have been mean to me!" I could hear the anger oozing out of her. I realized right away that she believed in the belief "How you treat others will come back to you, or they will mirror you." This belief is not completely true. I asked her, "But are you mean to yourself?" How you are with yourself is what you create, not how you treat others. You are the mold. She paused, and I could see the wheels turning inside her mind. After a long silence, she finally said, "You're right. I am very mean to me!" I could see this was a life-changing moment for this woman. My heart rejoiced to witness her free herself from truly unkind and unloving inner language.

THOUGHTS VERSUS BELIEFS

When it comes to creating anything in life, what I'm about to talk about is incredibly important and is usually the most misunderstood. I have people ask me, quite often, why they can't create something or why they keep creating the same things over and over again. I hear things like, "I meditate every day. I visualize it. I do my affirmations, but nothing changes."

The thoughts we think are not as powerful as the thoughts we believe. When I say "thoughts we believe," I'm talking about thoughts that you have believed from when you were young and most likely do not even realize you believe or hold within you as truth.

For example, it will not matter how many times you force yourself to say "I am abundant" or "I am wealthy" if your foundational beliefs are not having enough, lacking, experiencing scarcity, lacking self-control, living within your means, believing that money is the source of all evil, having a bad relationship with money, having a lack of respect for money, and so on. No daily mantra will trump your foundational beliefs. They are very strong and powerful even if not realized.

When I'm reading someone, I hear many conflicting beliefs. One I come across often is when someone is trying to find a job. If you hate the work but do it to survive, then it will be very hard for you to create a job. It's as if you're trying to head in two different directions. Whichever thought or belief is stronger within you will determine the time it takes to create—the need to pay the bills or the thought that "I'm burned out and can't force myself to do what I hate anymore." This will be different depending on how long you have forced yourself to do jobs you hate. How "good" (for lack of a better word, because I do not think this is actually good) are you at shutting down your inner pain and continuing to go in your current situation? I usually ask my client something like, "Well, which prayer do you want the universe to answer? You need a break, or you need a job?" Conflicting energies will slow down the creative process or even stop it.

This is why it is so important to do things in life that we love and that are in alignment with who we are as *beings*. So many times people will go after careers for the money, to be enough, important, or powerful, but they do not consider whether they love it or if it's their passion. Eventually this backfires into a conflict between "what I have to do because it's the only thing I know" and "I just can't do this anymore."

Listening to your intuition will create huge changes in your life if you honor it. Intuition is not a pipe dream. Intuition involves practical and step-by-step instructions in the now. When we honor and cultivate them, we make the most money and live the most fulfilling, happy lives. Yes, we all have many different gifts. Some people are architects, networkers, organizers, caregivers, healers, teachers, inventors, and so on.

Part of being congruent is honoring our inner voice. The other part is letting go of beliefs that do not support what we want to create. This can take time to realize, let go of, and create anew.

In readings, I'm always telling people what they need to let go of to create the lives they want. I'm never telling them they are lacking something. The ability to create love, a vocation, safety, and so on is there already. I'm reading what beliefs are blocking the person from creating them.

SATURATION

The level at which a person entertains thoughts is the level at which it affects the cell tissue. For example, some people may have a few stories they hold on to about structure (physical bones), and others may have many stories. I read a woman once who had been severely beaten as a child. Her bones showed me they were brittle and broke easily. The woman confirmed this was true. She had to be very careful because she was constantly breaking bones. When I read what created this, it was years of extreme structure. This started as a child with very strict rules about life, how to be, how to act, what to do and not do, and constant thoughts about the so-called proper way to be in life (structure). After years and years of trying to hold these beliefs up, the stress of carrying them affected and weakened her structure, which physically means her bones.

What your thoughts are about will determine what body part it affects. Depending on the number (saturation) of thoughts entertained about one topic, this will determine the severity and speed of ailment in the body.

HOW DOES IT SERVE YOU?

Another important topic that can be very sensitive is "How is it serving you?" There are several steps to letting go of beliefs:

1. Awareness
2. The decision to let go
3. A change in behavior

This is not as easy as you might think. I've witnessed people choose death over letting go of their stories. This is not good or bad, but it illustrates how powerful a belief can be. Using a story can be done in thousands of ways. Here is one example. Let's say you have been through a lot of emotional pain when it comes to romantic love. You could then use different stories to protect you from ever loving deeply again or allowing people to get close to you. You might constantly find things wrong with people. You might believe you are better off alone. You could believe all males or females are the same, and you just don't want anything to do with them. You could even decide that you are broken and unlovable. All these thoughts could be used to serve you in not allowing anyone close to you again.

Another example is this: due to trauma (stories), you have decided that you really don't want to live, you would rather just hide, or check out. There are then lots of thoughts that could support you in accomplishing not living, hiding, and checking out—stories like "I don't feel good"; "It's just the way it is, so why bother?"; "I don't want to heal"; "I don't deserve (or do deserve) whatever." If I suggested that you let go of these beliefs, why in the world would you want to do that if you consciously or unconsciously are using the stories to create what you want, which is to not live?

I would say as high as 99 percent of how beliefs serve us is unconscious. We do not realize what we are doing until someone suggests we let go. That suggestion will bring up all the reasons we want to hang on in the first place. Why you want to hang on is "how it is serving you." In order to be truly free, how it serves you will have to be healed or worked through first. Then it becomes easier to let go and change behavior.

Once you let go, the next step is a behavior change. This part can be very frustrating because we want to be different, but new patterns (habits) take patience and persistence to develop. It will do no good to beat yourself up if the changes do not happen automatically. Be gentle with yourself as old patterns lose their grips on you.

THE ILLUSION OF THE STORY...

Once, in a classroom, a woman said to me very emotionally that she was so sick of being alone. I was watching her emotions and the effects that believing she was alone were creating within her. This was not pleasant for her. I said to her, "But you're not alone!" Her emotions increased, and I watched her go into time (history) to explain why this thought was true. I listened to her and then said again, "But you're going through being alone because of believing your thoughts, when you're sitting in a room full of people."

I noticed two things as this was happening. One, as she entertained the thought of being alone, her thoughts were creating an experience that was not what was actually happening in reality. Two, as she believed the thought of being alone, she was also having all of the sensations that go along with it *depending* on her relationship with being alone.

We can have different relationships with beliefs. If she had been a person who loved her alone time and longed for it, making the statement, "I'm alone!" would have created a more pleasant experience within her. I realized that all energies are neutral, but we can have different relationships with them. Our relationship with the energy then determines our experience.

This helped me look at my relationship with "alone." First, is it even possible to be alone on a planet with seven billion people? Second, I noticed that when I believed the thought, it created me being disconnected from all that is. The thoughts, regardless of my relationship with them, created a focus on the thought versus the sense of being tied in to every living thing. Third, I realized I'm never alone because I always have me. When I'm truly hearing myself and showing up for myself in the moment, I do not feel alone.

One of our greatest powers, if not the greatest power, is deciding to believe a thought.

EVOLVING

I do not recommend that people do this work to become better. First of all, I do not believe there is anything wrong with you in the first place. I suggest you do this kind of work so that you can create the experience in life you want.

The word "evolve" does not mean getting better. It simply means "change." I also encourage you to take the word "lessons" out of your vocabulary when it comes to learning. You are not learning lessons as if you are bad or wrong. You are learning mind knowledge about different energies and what happens when you play with them in different ways. That is it. You are not getting better as a being because you are already more amazing than I could ever explain. You are only playing with different aspects of yourself. I say this because so many people approach this work and get disheartened because they "can't get it!" or they feel they're never enough. Please don't believe those thoughts or put yourself through that. Know that your magnificence far surpasses anything your mind could believe.

ONE THING LEADS TO ANOTHER

Of course one thing leads to another when you say yes and trust. Teaching these classes not only led to amazing relationships that played a huge role in my future but also to new territory. At this point in my learning, I believed that if you let the story go, the emotions would follow. I could see no reason there would be emotions in cell tissue that was unsupported by a story. One day I came across a man with severe **PTSD** from childhood. I did my usual speech: "If you let go of the story, there is nothing to support the sensations." He *slammed* his fist down on the table; when he spoke, his voice had almost a growl in it. "The sensations I have in my body from my stepfather raping me are real sensations that come out of nowhere!"

The room got very quiet. I heard him. I could see what he was describing was real for him. I also only knew what I knew. Maybe he knew something I didn't. His passion and insistence created a pause in me. "I don't have answers for you, but I hear you. I hear what you are saying, and I believe you." This opening in me took many years to bloom into wisdom.

CHAPTER 5

Discovering New Tools

❧

ALTHOUGH I WAS TEACHING AND experiencing an advanced level of intuition, my personal life and inner world were a mess. Looking back now, writing this, I can clearly see how I was in such distress. I was carrying emotional history and was aware of my pain, but I couldn't figure out how to free myself from it.

During the energy education classes, I met people who opened up new opportunities. One was a volunteer program called the Jessie Program. The program was designed to help young girls between the ages of fourteen and eighteen make transitions from juvenile detention back into society. In the beginning, I just wanted to support the program because my schedule was already overbooked, but as time went on, I got more and more sucked into the program. The director of the program was an amazing woman. Her drive and passion were contagious. As the months went on, I ended up helping with fundraisers, training, interviewing possible new mentors, and eventually going into the hall every other week to teach the girls about thought patterns. We were not allowed to take even staples into the detention center. I would take one piece of paper for each girl that would have my lesson plan. Each week, I would do my best to help them break down unsupportive thoughts that they believed and reach for thoughts that supported them in creating the lives they wanted to live.

Anytime I am in an extreme energy, it is easier for me to read. This happened in the emergency department, and it happened with the girls. Their thoughts and emotional pain were so strong, it was easy for me to read and come to understand why they were creating the things in life they were creating. This taught me how important our core foundational beliefs really are. It also hit me hard because I had not stopped long enough to look at my foundation or my emotional pain.

During this time of my life, I was a mess. I was working full time as a vice president/officer at a bank. I supervised a large team that managed all of the bank's construction loans within the United States, and I worked at least ten hours a day, six days a week. In addition, I was doing research in the ED with Dr. Karen, volunteering at the Jessie Program, teaching energy education classes, raising a son, trying to have a relationship with Dennis (which was starting to have problems), and completely not hearing the pain going on inside me. I was still smoking weed to shut down and on occasion drinking way too much with friends. I was so lost! I used running nonstop to avoid my pain. It was so frustrating to see the things I saw intuitively, know that I had worked on myself for years, and yet still feel so much pain inside. If I just kept going, then maybe I would get there. I wasn't sure where "there" was, but I was sure trying to get there.

What I learned during this time while teaching the girls within the hall was that I was not able to apply or change my behavior overnight. In fact, it took me years to fully change my inner world and behavior, and that naturally changed my outer world.

FOUNDATION

While working with the girls, I started to notice what was missing from their foundations—meaning the key things we need that help us create life: relationships, careers, homes, self-care, and financial stability.

During this timeframe, I wrote a workbook titled *Write Your Own Story*. It helps you let go of sabotaging thoughts and embrace thoughts that support you in creating the life you want to live. I've been asked several times to write an adult version of this workbook, but the truth is, the workbook is an adult version. Without the cartoon pictures, the information within the workbook is what a person would need to do at any age to change his or her foundation.

Within the workbook, I use a house to illustrate your life. If you were going to draw a blueprint of the life you want, what would that look like? Each room symbolizes career, life partner, children, hobbies, service, friendships, spirituality, travel, learning, and so on. When building a house, the blueprint of the house tells you what will be needed within the foundation: where the plumbing pipes go, the different elevations, where the footings go, and so on. Your life blueprint is the same. It tells you what you need in your foundation in order to create the things you want in life.

Let's say you want a deep, loving relationship. You would need a deep, loving relationship with yourself first. The level at which you love yourself determines the level of love you are able to receive and create. *Remember, you are the mold, and you create what you are!* You may want a mate who would protect you. Then you would need to protect yourself. You may want this person to be loyal. Then you would need to be loyal to yourself (loyal to your inner voice, intuition, and feelings). You may want this person to hear you. Then you would need to hear yourself. You probably want to be able to trust this person. Then you would need to trust yourself. (Trust that you would protect yourself. Trust that you would not hurt yourself. Trust that you would hear yourself. Trust that you will work hard at your life. Trust that you will show up for yourself.) I'm sure you are starting to see what I'm saying. Look at what you want to create, and then ask what would be needed in a foundation to create it. Your foundation is *you*!

What if you wanted to create a career? A career may require education, advancement in a company, and the courage to follow your gifts and passions. Your foundation would need courage, discipline, self-love, rest, knowledge, focus, emotional support, perseverance, drive, ambition, dedication, willingness, and patience!

After you have created a life blueprint, then go back to each room (symbolic of what you wanted to create in life), and determine what would be needed in the foundation to manifest that in life.

Very quickly, I came to understand that love is the core component that supports everything else. If you do not love yourself and your life, you will not do things like protect yourself, care for yourself, work hard for yourself, or not do things that hurt yourself. This may sound easy. Usually people are very quick to say, "Okay, okay, I love myself!" without really looking at decisions they make, the way they talk to themselves, how they treat themselves, how they allow others to treat them, or if they are valuable enough, in their own eyes, to do the work.

You will try to obtain from outside sources what you do not have in your foundation. If you do not love yourself, you will try to get love from outside sources, even to a point that you are not loving yourself. It's as if you are saying, "Love me more than I'm willing to love myself. I will let you hurt me and treat me horribly to get love from you." This is a very painful life to live. When you love yourself, needing love from outside sources changes to sharing love.

The young adults I was working with had so much missing from their foundations that it was impossible for them to create lives. They spent most of their time trying to satisfy their needs from outside sources: love, belonging, worth, acceptance, happiness, support, trust, safety, importance, nurturing, parenting, and so much more. Most of them had no idea how to create these characteristics within themselves. I looked at why their foundations didn't have these necessary characteristics. I would see it was taught or not taught— taught by behavior, decisions, and beliefs of people around them. Their inner language and actions did not have self-love. Their thoughts involved words like the following: not enough, not important, blame, not fair, unworthy, unloved, bad, stupid, ugly, lost, didn't belong, unwanted, uncared for, a burden, neglected, abandoned, misfits, and broken. How in the world could you create an amazing life with a foundation that had self-hate, loathing, and burdens in it?

I knew they were valuable, smart, important, and enough. If I just told them they were these things, they didn't believe me because their thoughts and history told them otherwise. So first, I helped them let go of thoughts that were untrue about themselves and life. I did this by questioning their current thoughts. I did this with them each week. I show how to do this, step by step, within the workbook *Write Your Own Story*. Letting go of unsupportive thoughts did not just happen overnight but started to create cracks in their foundations. Cracks were good because if they could break up and remove the foundations that disempowered them, then they could replace it with thoughts that did support them—new foundations!

As the new thoughts were introduced, at first it made no sense to them. "Support me! Okay, *how*?" or "Trust me! Okay, *how*?" What does that even mean? I had to figure out a way to illustrate what this looked like in thoughts, actions, and decisions. I realized it was easy for them to tell me how they would give these things to other people. I would ask them to make a list of how they support a friend, parent, child, or girlfriend/boyfriend. Then I would tell them to go through each item listed and ask if they gave it to themselves and to start doing that. We did the same with all characteristics they needed to develop. Let's use trust as an example. I would ask them to make a list of how they created trust with a friend, parent, child, or girlfriend/boyfriend. Then I would say, "Now turn each thing on your list around, and ask if you provide these things for you." We did it over and over again on each characteristic: importance, worth, value, caring, nurturing, love, belonging, and many more.

Another very important topic was parenting themselves. In many cases, their parents were absent or nonexistent. They were stuck in what I term "parentlessness." (But many people do not have parents and function just fine.) Whether you are five or forty-five when your parents leave or die, you step into parenting yourself. This idea was new to them but changed and supported them greatly. There is also the huge question of how to parent you. Are you a loving, supportive parent or a parent who is harsh and disinterested? Learning how to parent yourself in a positive, supportive, and empowering way takes time and is needed in a person's foundation.

Working with the young adults made me start to realize things. One was that I didn't believe I was important. I tried so hard in the outside world to be important, but my health wasn't important, hearing my emotional pain wasn't important, protecting myself wasn't important, working at a healthy level wasn't important, and so on. Most of my decisions, thoughts, and actions showed how unimportant my precious life was to me. As I read all these things within these amazing young *beings*, it forced me to look at my programming from childhood. What thoughts did I still entertain that made me feel horrible, made me hurt myself, and created me not loving my life to the fullest extent?

For the most part, we are not taught that it is our responsibility to generate and maintain our own happiness, safety, self-nurturing, self-love, self-importance, self-worth, and thousands more characteristics. We are taught to look to outside sources for most, if not all, of our needs. That creates us being slaves to those sources just to get our needs met. This is too much to expect from another human being. Self-care and being selfish are two very different things! With self-care, you do not expect others to give you things that really only can be sustained by you.

There is a difference between sharing and needing. When you need something such as love, attention, safety, importance, or acceptance from another person, then you are a slave to that person to get your need met. You give that person your power. When you *share* characteristics with someone, there is no power struggle. This is very important. Many times in life, especially with our mates, we will share the generating of characteristics. Maybe a man generates more safety and the woman generates more nurturing, but it's not because they can't or *need* the other person to do this.

It's how they share creating life together. Although the difference may seem subtle, it is actually huge.

I came to understand how crucial the foundation is. It determines how we talk to ourselves; it determines the decisions we make or don't make, our actions, and health. This is also one of the hardest things to change because it feels normal to each person when it's all he or she knows. Our first foundation in life is mainly created for us as we are raised. Most people are unconscious of what is in their foundation. It takes self-reflection and patience to change programming that happened when we were very young.

JACKHAMMERING MY FOUNDATION

I started a long road of dismantling my life, as if I were jackhammering my foundation so that I could build anew. The demolition stage was not fun. I didn't really know what I was doing, but I knew my life had to change in order to be in alignment with who I was as a being. My career was slowly killing me but made me feel important, accomplished, financially stable, and successful. When I started to generate thoughts that I was important, accomplished, stable, and successful within me, I didn't need the unhealthy career to give me what I had been missing. Yes, I needed to work, but what was my vocation in life? What was my passion? What gift did I have to give to this world? This did not happen overnight. It took many years. In fact, without realizing it, I had already begun working on my vocation. It just hadn't gotten to the point of supporting me financially yet. I didn't have the energy to weave into moving my vocation forward because I was too busy trying to be important and accomplished at a career I hated. As I changed my energy investment, my life changed.

This also changed my relationship with Dennis. One of the most heartbreaking changes was labeling our relationship what it really was: best friends. We were best friends. I had no idea how to live without him, but we were not in love anymore. It was god-awful accepting this and doing what was needed to separate. I wanted to be deeply in love with someone. I wanted a partner who shared my same passions in life. It had become clear that although Dennis and I played a huge role in each other's lives, our relationship as mates had come to an end. As I stated at the beginning of this chapter, looking at my foundation and what my heart truly wanted created huge devastating changes within my life. It took courage and time to align my life with what truly honored me.

Also, at this time, my son went away to school in Arizona. So many things in my life that were my identity came to an end all at once. My corporate career, my relationship, and my son moving away were the start of a very new, scary road for me. I was not a butterfly yet. At this point, I was in the cocoon learning to connect with myself deeper, and I was healing.

BREATH RELEASE

What I'm about to share next is very important. If you miss this part of the book, you will not understand why I come back to this as a lifeline. Around this time, a couple of friends introduced me to breath release. I listened to the experiences they described, and although it sounded scary, it obviously was having a huge impact on them. I was desperate to heal myself and stop hurting. Since I was a child, at least twice a year, I would get group A strep throat. Strep can affect your vital organs and be very dangerous if untreated. The Breath Release sessions were held in an individual's home. You breathe really fast for an hour. I can't remember everything I went through during those original sessions, but you can cramp up really bad in your hands and feet, people are screaming and crying in the room, you go into an altered state, and so much more. I only went about five or six times before I had a life-changing, extremely scary experience. It was toward the end of the session. I started to see in my mind's eye when I was a little girl. My dad would spank me, but if I cried or screamed, I would get another spanking. I remember trying so hard not to make any noise. I also saw many times in my life that it was not okay to speak or to have a voice. As all of this was being shown to me, I was coughing and gagging. My throat felt heavier and heavier, and then the sensation of a huge tumor, larger than my throat, was slowly being pulled out of me. It was so physically real that I could feel the cell tissue separating as it was being pulled up and out of me. It felt like it was lifting my upper body off the mat, which it actually was. I could feel the mass separate out of me, and then I fell back down gently onto the mat. Once this session was over, I was so completely petrified that I stopped going to breath sessions. About eighteen months later, it occurred to me that I had not gotten strep throat in a long time. I started to think about it and realized that the last time I had strep throat was actually prior to this experience of the energetic mass being removed from my throat. I have never had strep throat again.

Even after I realized the huge impact the breath sessions had had on me, I was still unwilling to do it again. There was still more spiraling out of control before I got desperate enough to do anything and everything.

SECOND CONTACT

A second contact that I made while doing the energy education classes led me to work with people over the phone. I discovered I really enjoyed working with people over the phone because it was easier for me to focus on their energy without a body sitting in front of me. When I read people, I see them at many different ages. I referred to these as anchors.

I was talking to a client in her late forties over the phone. She was describing an emotion she kept experiencing. Regardless of how hard she tried, she couldn't figure out why she felt this way or how to stop it. I could see her at different ages as she talked to me. Without thinking, I asked her, "As you talk about this, how old do you feel?"

She paused for an inner reflective moment and then said, "I don't know, maybe eighteen or nineteen."

I asked her, "Is that the first time you felt this emotion, or did it start younger?" I could see what she was talking about around eighteen or nineteen, but the origin happened when she was about three. I could see this little three-year-old girl feeling what she had just described to me.

She said, "No, I guess if I think about it, I'm a lot younger. Maybe three or four."

I said, "Okay. Tell me what the little girl (you) looks like."

The client said, "She is very pale. Her dress is kind of ragged and dirty. Her face is dirty. She just looks down." (I could see what see was talking about as she described it.) "Which is completely typical of my childhood. No one really paid much attention to me or cared if I had a bath or had eaten. I was completely neglected." I could hear the anger, hurt, and hate in her voice, which were the emotions she had been feeling and couldn't stop feeling.

I slowed things way down so I could hear my intuitive direction because I didn't know what to do or say. I knew from my work with the young girls in juvenile hall that you couldn't change or fix the past. It had already happened and was over. The only place the event was still happening was within the person's mind, which is incredibly powerful. I knew that this event was no longer happening, but what was keeping it alive? I wondered what would happen if her adult self had a conversation with her three-year-old self.

So I instructed her. "Can you enter the picture within your mind as your adult self (the age you are now), and go up to your three-year-old self?"

The client paused, and I could feel her trying to see this within her mind. Then she said, "Yes, I can!"

"Awesome! Tell me what she is doing when she sees you!"

The client said, "Nothing really. She looks puzzled."

"Okay, I want you to go up to her and kneel down to her level and then say, 'I'm you all grown up. I've come to talk to you.'" I paused and waited for her to do this. What was cool for me was that I could see and feel her doing it. After waiting a few minutes, I said, "Tell me what she is doing."

The client said, "She is not really doing anything. Just standing, looking at me."

"What does she feel like to you? What emotions do you feel in her? If she was your daughter, how would you approach her?" I was trying to give her different ways to engage with her younger self.

The client said, "She seems surprised that I am talking to her. She is bashful maybe even a little uncomfortable."

Then it hit me. Her parents and people she grew up with were no longer neglecting her other than within her mind. The only person who could possibly still be doing this behavior to her was herself. The light bulb went on.

I said, "Ask her if she feels heard by you!"

The client didn't even have time to do the instruction. She started to cry. She already knew the answer. Crying, she said, "I know I don't listen to myself."

"Okay, but ask her anyway, and hear what she has to say."

The client said, "Do I listen to you?" I could see the woman kneeling before this little girl, sincerely asking this question and listening.

There were several moments of silence. I could feel the woman struggling with this. I finally said, "What is she doing?"

The client said, "Nothing really. She is just standing there not saying anything and looking at me with a blank look on her face. I'm not sure what do to or say to her."

"It's okay. Say this to her: 'I'm sorry I haven't listened to you. I'm sorry I haven't heard you or talked to you, but I promise I will start now. I can't promise I will do it perfectly, but I can promise I will start to try. I want you to know that you are special to me, and I will slow down and listen to you.'"

I gave this woman a very long time to process it, soak in the apology, and bond with her inner self. At times, it was hard for me to be patient and allow the client time to go through everything she needed to go through in order to let go, find peace, and commit to be different. It was such a huge realization. It doesn't matter what others did to us in the past; what matters is whether we are still doing it to ourselves in the now. Many times we are taught these things, but it is we who keep them alive by continuing to do them: treating ourselves certain ways, talking to ourselves certain ways, and doing the same behaviors. What heals us is not others being different, but us being different.

We spent weeks going back to this scenario and doing inner work. During our sessions, many promises were made to treat herself differently, such as the following:

Trust. "I know you don't trust me because I have not listened to you. I have not protected you. I have loved others over you. I have not nourished you but starved you. I have hated you and picked you apart. I have given you hundreds of reasons not to trust me, but I want you to know I'm trying not to do that anymore to you. I hear you. I want to keep you safe. I will love you over men in my life. I will feed you healthy food so you are not hungry. I will talk lovingly to you and stop pointing out what I think is wrong with you. Please trust that I am trying until you can trust me completely."

Belonging. "I know I have not made you feel welcome. I've made you uncomfortable in your own body by harassing you, critiquing you, and being mean to you. I have not created a warm, safe environment inside myself that feels like home to you. It is not true that you do not belong or are too different. I make you feel so uncomfortable you want to climb out of your skin, and for that I am so sorry. You belong! You are different in all the perfect ways to be you. I'm sorry I have made you feel unwelcome and like such an outcast. I am sorry I didn't love you. Please forgive me as I try to create an inner world of home, love, and safety for you. A place that you want to reside in. A place where you belong."

Abandonment. "I'm sorry I have abandoned you. I'm sorry I have checked out of my life, run nonstop, and never considered your feelings. I abandoned hearing you. I abandoned taking your best interests to heart. I abandoned protecting you. I abandoned how you feel. I'm so sorry I abandoned you. Please forgive me as I start to show up in your life, care about what you think, feel, and say. I promise to start embracing you with love, protection, and acceptance."

INTEGRATION

After many treatments with different phone clients, it occurred to me one day there should be no separation between the adult self and all the different ages I could see in people. One day I tried a new technique. After a client had made the commitment, I asked the client to absorb the younger self into the solar plexus area. A particular client was able to do this. I brought the client back into the current moment and asked this client to look back at the picture and see if it was empty or if the younger self could still be seen there. Most of the time, the client would declare the picture was empty. This told me that a true integration had happened. If the client could still see himself or herself there, or if later the client could see himself or herself there again, this told me there was still more work to do. More self-healing!

Along with phone readings came invitations to speak. I would lecture and then see clients all day long. Finally, I started to see how this could be practical and plausible in my life as a career.

PTSD LOOP: JOHN

While on a trip, I met a wonderful thirty-two-year-old man named John. From the time he was eight, he had suffered with migraines. He came to me very skeptical and desperate. His social anxiety and the impact migraines had on his life were significant. I assisted John in going back to the events that happened when he was eight. The trauma was a huge story for John. In many ways, he was using it as a barrier to not allow people close to him. He felt scared when people got close to him, and his story protected him. His story was constantly present with him. This was the first time I could see what I call a PTSD loop. Over and over again, the movie of what happened in his life at eight would play in his head like it was stuck on repeat. There was resistance in John during the first session to let go of the story or to look at the story any differently, but I must say that his openness to do the session was an act of being very brave.

In the first session, he accomplished cleaning up the past memories but didn't quite get to how he was treating himself. The next day John called me, and I could hear the panic in his voice. He said he had a migraine and a really bad one. We made arrangements for him to come right over for another session. During the second session, we were able to look at whether he was mean to himself, protected himself, heard himself, was gentle with himself, and hated himself. Anything he felt like an outside source had done to him when he was little was now doing to himself. At the end of the second session, John was able to integrate his younger self into his body. He left, and I didn't hear from John for a couple of years.

One day out of the blue, I got a message he wanted to talk. Since we lived in different states, we made arrangements to have a phone conversation. It was a pleasure to hear from him. He started out by telling me he had experienced no migraines since our prior sessions. My heart rejoiced for

John. He said his social anxiety had improved greatly also. But in order to get married at a particular location, he and his fiancée started to go to counseling. In so doing, his migraines had remanifested. I knew right away that what he had healed and let go of during our sessions had been opened back up. So for thirty minutes, I worked over the phone with John to let go and clear out any behavior he was doing to trigger the story. Since then I have stayed in contact with John, and he is doing well.

TELEPATHIC WHAT?

My intuition continued to grow with or without me being prepared for it. I had left the corporate world but still needed to supplement my income with private accounting clients. One day while at a job site, up in the attic where the office was located, I had a horrifying experience that led to a breakthrough for me. My dad appeared energetically before me. He was standing in front of the desk but not saying anything to me. My heart came up in my throat. I rolled the chair back away from the desk and started to panic and cry. My thoughts were, "Oh my God, my dad passed away." My first thought was to call Dennis because he knew and understood my experiences with intuition. As soon as he heard my cracking voice, he said seriously, "April, what's wrong?"

"I think my dad died. He just appeared right in front of me. He didn't say anything. It was like he was checking on me, and then he was gone." I was very emotional and distraught.

Dennis replied, "Well call your mom, and find out what's going on."

Now remember, I was disowned when I was nineteen years old. Yes, I had talked to my parents here and there over the years, but calling them was not something I usually did. Regardless, I dialed my mom. In my head I was trying to calm myself so she didn't think anything was wrong. I had no idea what she knew or didn't know at this point.

She answered, and trying my best to sound normal I asked her, "Mom, is Dad home?"

She said, "April, what's wrong?" (I laugh at this now because of course my mom could tell I was upset, even though I was trying to hide it.)

"Everything is fine, Mom. Is Dad home?"

She replied, "No, he isn't home yet from work, but he should be home within the next fifteen minutes."

I said, "Okay. As soon as he walks in the door, please have him call me."

I sat there crying, trying to figure out what could have happened to him. Did his heart give out? I concluded that I was too emotionally close to the situation to read it correctly. My phone rang, and the caller ID read Mom. I answered, and much to my surprise I heard my dad's voice. I almost burst into tears and then had to come up with a reason for calling him out of the blue.

Relieved but puzzled, I decided to go home. Feeling emotionally drained after the strange experience, I couldn't stop thinking about how strongly he had manifested in front of me. Late that night in bed, it hit me like a ton of bricks. "What is the difference between talking to someone in the physical form versus someone that is not?" That thought had never occurred to me. What is the difference? Why would there be any difference? A being is a being. Oh my God, so why can't I talk to beings in form just like I can beings that are not in form? I don't know. I never tried. Talking to beings not in form was never my favorite thing to do. In fact, I avoided it. I wasn't sure how I felt about all of this, but I couldn't stop thinking about it all night.

The next day in the ED with patients, I tried to telepathically talk to them. It felt weird, and I didn't quite know what I was doing, but I could connect a little. I wasn't sure if I wanted to get better at it, but I was definitely fascinated with thinking about it. I wondered if it would help me read people faster. Instead of profiling their emotions, thoughts, and cell tissue, maybe I could just ask them what was wrong with them. Interesting thought! This started a six-to-eight-month exploration of telepathically connecting with people. Once I worked through my fears and discomfort with it, I started to enjoy it. Reading people was faster, extremely accurate, and even brutally honest.

CHAPTER 6

Time Traveling to Suffer

⚜

AS MY IDENTITY DEFINED AS career, relationship, and the moving away of my son dissolved, I was left with only myself. I didn't realize how uncomfortable I was with myself. Acting like a rebellious teenager, I labeled it being open and going with the flow. In truth, I was completely out of control. I didn't want to be with just me. So I ran around drinking up anything that numbed me or made me feel better. I was smoking weed all of the time. My drinking was increasing as my going out increased. I found great amounts of joy several times a week in dancing, which became a huge part of my life. I was living off my 401(k) and savings. I justified this behavior to myself with lots of excuses. I had never really partied or dated in my twenties. I was busy being a mother, working, and creating a life. Now I just wanted to let my hair down, be out of control, and pretty much do nothing. I didn't realize that the truth was I was burnt out, discouraged, and hurting.

I wasn't important enough to my own self to work hard anymore. (I was willing to work really hard in life when I had my son with me. He was worth it to me, but now it was just me.) I was unwilling to work hard at life for just myself. So I did not.

I dated some very successful men during this time. Sex and dating were great ways to escape my inner pain. I dated the son of a foreign president for about eight months and then a retired professional football player. Life was crazy. I was crazy. Now, looking back, I can see I was attracting people into my life that were just as lost and confused about the next chapter in life, and they were trying to numb their pain. I was destroying friendships and making new friends who were not healthy. The journey inside myself was not smooth. It was a bumpy ride down, to say the least.

And then...the bait came into my life. As if you had put weights around my ankles and dropped me in deep water, I met what would sink me. The final nail in the coffin! A man! We will call him Gavlin. Let me be clear—it was not Gavlin who sank me but what he brought up in me that did.

I was out dancing one night, and from the dance floor I turned around, and there he stood. The most beautiful being I had ever seen. He was also the largest energetic being I had ever seen—the size of the entire back wall. He was standing in front of a set of French doors. The sun was setting, and it made his energy (being) glow brilliantly. Yes, he is a handsome man in the physical form, but his being was magnificent to me. I stopped dancing and walked straight up to him. He watched me approach, and I said, "You are the largest being I have ever seen. Your energy is amazing!"

When he heard what I had said, he seemed surprised and then quite proud of himself. I'm sure most men would love to hear what big beings they are. This was not love at first sight. It was as if I had always loved this man, even before I met him. I have never felt such a connection with someone, such deep, unconditional love—a sense of being telepathically connected, a sense of belonging. I was starving for belonging. It was like a drug, breathing him in, that I could not get enough of.

I came to find out that he loved to Latin dance. I started going out several times a week salsa dancing. Gradually I started to learn several different types of Latin dancing. This fed me in ways I needed, but again, I did it in an out-of-control way.

This is not the perfect fairy tale. Gavlin was a brilliant man, retired military, who suffered from extreme PTSD after having been in three wars. He struggled with using vices to make the memories and emotional sensations better and had given up on ever healing himself. He would say to me, "April, I'm dead!"

I could see people who had passed over to the other side around him that he was hanging onto. I would tell him what they said to me in hopes he would forgive himself. He told me many times he was broken beyond repair, that he deserved the life he lived, and he didn't want me to try to help him heal. Of course, I didn't listen. I didn't want to just let him drown. Unknowingly, it was easier to focus on him than me.

We would go long periods without seeing each other. He would drop off the face of the earth into a bottle, into his own pain and into the arms of other women or whatever numbed the torture he experienced inside his body. Yes, as I write this, I am aware of how crazy I sound. I would write him love letters trying to reach him and save him. I thought while he went into his hole that if he had something to read and knew someone loved him, he might possibly start to love himself. It was heart wrenching and god-awful what I put myself through—yes, I put myself through this. Gavlin was doing what he was supposed to be: learning, experiencing, processing, and healing. It was my opinion that he was supposed to be somewhere other than where he was. I was the one out of alignment with reality. I was the one who thought it should have been different. In this act of rejection of what was/is, I got stuck in the illusion of time. I dug my heels in and refused to move because reality was that hard for me to accept. I wanted my story. I wanted my way. Me shutting down was an act of punishing the universe in some childish way: "Fine. You're not going to give me what I want, so I just won't live." This is what I mean by saying that I put myself through it.

I remember telling Dr. Karen who had become a dear friend, "This man is going to introduce me to the devil, but I don't care. I have to do this. I'm in love with him, and I don't care. I just know this is something I have to do." I was right; it was something I had to do to plunge deep inside myself. At the time, I didn't understand what was happening. He did introduce me to the devil—my devil inside me that needed to be healed.

Trying to save him resulted in me being obsessed with researching military PTSD. I would profile the psyches of military clients for hours. As I figured out different helpful ideas, I would share them in love letters to Gavlin. If I could just figure it out, then maybe I could save him from his pain, and we could be together. The truth was I wanted to save myself and be able to love him, because I did love him, I just didn't love myself. I was just as scared as he was and was just as petrified to allow someone close to me. I was running just as much as he was. In thousands of ways, we were mirroring each other, neither of us realizing it at the time!

It's hard to honor a connection with someone else when you can't even stand to be connected to your own self. Starving to connect is really the desire to be connected to one's own self. I felt so disconnected. I'm now able to articulate it, but at the time, I just felt lost, scared, angry, confused, and petrified to not figure it out and exhausted from trying to always get there but never being able to. I kept going, numbing, pushing myself, and checking out.

STEPPING UP THE GAME

For years, I had been working with clients on how to let go of stories. Now I was faced with more powerful traumatic stories along with many added elements that go with PTSD: migraines, insomnia, anxiety, depression, isolation, addictions, neurological issues, nightmares, flashbacks, and being overwhelmed constantly.

I did what I have always done: trusted my intuition in the moment as I worked with military men and women. As was the case many times in my life when profiling anything extreme, it was easier for me to sense and understand. I started to ask two questions: what creates stories being stuck within a person, and what determines how often we think of those stories?

While analyzing these questions, I remembered many years ago my friend asking me, "Why do you always see the negative in people when reading them?" All these years, her statement has stuck with me. I would hear her in my head asking me why I always see the negative.

When I hear something within my mind over and over again and for several years, it is because it has importance. Sometimes it takes me years to figure it out and understand why. Once I got over my own judgment of myself, I was able to look at it objectively. That last sentence is important! The answers were always there, but I didn't ask the questions. I was stuck in self-judgment of being negative or positive. There was a time I thought, "Oh, my God, am I creating it by thinking it!" When I talk about blocks a person has to work through, this is what I mean.

So why do I only see the negative while profiling? That is actually a very good question. The answer that came to me was this: "I can't see it if a person is not holding onto it or actively thinking about it in this moment." For example, people do not walk around carrying their wedding days with them, but if they are thinking about them in the moment, I can feel that.

The next logical question was this: what creates a person holding onto certain stories? I noted that the stronger the hold on the story, the easier it was for me to see. But what was creating the hold? If you're not holding on to experiences in life, then they just flow through you. What stops the flow? The answer I got was profound: *the flow stops when we reject, block, or suppress experiences in life.* This is incredibly important when it comes to healing. It is not the emotions or thoughts that create the illness but the holding on to them. I will use love as an example. Most people hold love in high regard, but if they block the flow of love within the heart, it will create blockages in the heart. I started to understand the importance of our relationship with energies. Our relationship with energies determines whether we allow them to flow through us.

So the answer to my friend's question is this: "If you're not holding onto it, I can't see it! Outside of your mind, it doesn't exist."

A person's relationship with energies unconsciously is molded from what his or her experience in life has been with that energy: love, anger, frustration, and hurt. The relationship we currently have with a particular energy is not set in stone. It can be chiseled and refined. You can create a new relationship by letting go of any blocks that keep it from flowing through you.

Both Gavlin and I really struggled with the energy of love. Although we were both starved for it, we were also petrified of it. This created us getting super close and then running away. Neither of us had any idea how to be okay with love in our bodies. I remember I said to him one day, "Is it ever going to be okay to love you?" I asked this because my love for him seemed to make him uncomfortable. He didn't believe he deserved it, or that I would stay with him. Equally, I was also scared—scared he would never really love me or stay with me. We were so busy creating our fears that there was no way we could have created a relationship.

REWRITING THE STORY

Up until this point, I was taking people into their stories and assisting them in letting go. This level of attachment I saw symbolically as a meat hook within them or an anchor keeping them stuck. Now I was working with military clients who had extreme PTSD. I symbolically saw huge trenches of which people could not climb out. In Western medicine, there is the term "neurological pathways." Extreme trauma creates these neuro pathways to become like trenches. It can feel impossible to get out of. Imagine being in a trench that is twice as deep as your height; the walls are slick with mud, and you are already exhausted. The despair and helplessness consume you. Due to exhaustion and not knowing what to do, it becomes easier to create a home down there in the trench and give up trying to get out. Of course my next logical question was, "How do you level the trench?"

You cannot just fill in the trench. This is how most people, in the beginning, try to approach their trauma. Doing this is like covering over dead bodies with dirt. It will pollute the water and ground so that it is unhealthy and unlivable. Covering over your trauma, ignoring it, staying busy, or using denial will pollute your mind, emotional body, and physical cell tissue. It will make your body feel like you can't live in it anymore.

It took about six to eight months of working with military clients to intuitively find solutions. I kept listening to my intuitive guidance in each session, and all of a sudden, clients started to report experiences of healing. Later, I had to go back and figure out why. What I was being told to do worked, but how to put it into language was hard.

I remember getting the impression to slowly scrape the edges of the trench away and put it on the bottom of the trench. This made the trench wider, and the bottom began to rise. The trench originally was deep and narrow because it was a very ingrained story that didn't change much. My clients with extreme PTSD would explain to me that their flashbacks and thoughts about the situation were basically the same over and over again. I helped them broaden the story (trench) by adding to the story or seeing it in different ways.

For example, let's say the story goes something like this: "Myself and a fellow brother (marine) were out late on patrol. We hit an IED. The vehicle flipped on its side, and I was knocked unconscious. When I came to, I was hanging by my seat belt. I released the belt and fell down onto my fellow brother, who was dead. I couldn't see. I felt my way to climb up and out of the vehicle. I could smell fire, which created some light, but my eyes were blurry, and I could only see fuzzy shapes in the darkness. Once I managed to climb up and out; then I had to jump down without being able to see. I knew the jump had to be at least twenty feet down. I jumped! Broke my ankle and crawled away from the vehicle that was being consumed in fire. I will never forget the smell."

The story above creates a narrow, deep trench. But what happens to the trench if you add to the story or change it? It widens! This is how you add to a story or change it:

1. Can you see yourself being too sick to go out on patrol and staying in the barracks?
2. Can you see yourself dying instead of your fellow brother?
3. Can you see driving a different route and then driving back to the barracks?
4. Can you see yourself driving?
5. Can you see both of you living?
6. Can you see you losing an arm?
7. Can you see the car jump up and over the IED? (Sure, make it fly in the air!)

As you see the story in different ways, it widens the trench and creates the PTSD loop to dissolve. A very important part of this technique is to see and feel each scenario as if it happened that way. Above are seven different ways to recreate the story, but to be effective, you will need to go slowly through each scenario with as many different outcomes as you can think of. I started to refer to this technique as rewriting the story.

The results were shocking. Clients started reporting that their ailments were gradually disappearing or were gone—ailments like flashbacks, migraines, insomnia, digestive issues, being overwhelmed, anxiety, social stress, isolation, and much more.

The mental part of the trauma was healing, but the visceral sensations were still there. I kept hearing feedback describing the story not playing in their head over and over again and when they looked at the story (traumatic event), it seemed murky and not as clear BUT they were still experiencing sensations that would just hit them out of the blue.

THE EMOTIONAL BODY

When clients described these sensations, I intuitively saw them as different colors all woven into their cell tissue. It got brighter and louder once I noticed it and started to pay attention to it. I didn't know what "it" was. It looked like different colors of fog saturated throughout the cell tissue.

I remembered the passionate/insistent man who had been raped by his stepfather who had said to me, "The sensations I have in my body...are real sensations that come out of nowhere!"

I started to refer to what I was seeing as the emotional body. I had no idea how to access it or move it out of the body.

WHY WE STOP OURSELVES FROM HEALING

Compiling all this data was becoming a book on military PTSD, which I had planned to title *Time Traveling to Suffer*. I gave the book outline to Gavlin in love letters. I thought in order for Gavlin to help himself, he would have to first work through why he didn't want to get better and heal. I have never found just one reason that people stop themselves from healing, but rather many reasons, and they all feed off of each other.

Here are a few reasons:

1. You are angry with yourself or others, so you think, "Just fuck it!"
2. You are stuck in self-punishment.
3. You are scared to live anymore, and the story protects you from having to live.
4. You are afraid you can never truly heal and will always see the things you see in your head.
5. You are not brave enough to look at yourself or the trauma.
6. You are refusing to be accountable.
7. You are scared that if you let the story go, then you will do it again.
8. You think, "It's my cross to bear." You refuse to forgive yourself.
9. You are holding on to stories to keep people alive that you lost.
10. You are too tired to even live, let alone do the work needed to heal.
11. You think, "I deserve this!"

There are thousands of reasons why we sabotage ourselves from healing. Realizing how our pain serves us is always the first obstacle to overcome in order to heal.

HITTING BOTTOM

Healing myself was no different. I was not willing to let go of my stories or be accountable yet, even though I was suffering and in constant self-destruct mode. I believed I could manage or maintain it, but I was lying to myself.

There was no good way for the situation between Gavlin and me to end. In fact, it never really ended. We were both on such a crash course, and the wreckage took over and got in the way of us being together. He was doing exactly what I needed him to do, which was bringing up all of my deepest fears: belonging, abandonment, being enough, and hurt. I just kept numbing more and more, running from my pain like a car going ninety miles an hour, and then I hit a brick wall.

Finally I hit bottom! One night, while out dancing, I got myself into a situation in which I was physically and sexually assaulted. The trauma I went through that night was my end. There was no more road for me. I was done. During the assault, I started to pray for death. For many months, that prayer stayed with me. Daily, I prayed for death. In the beginning, I drank several bottles of wine every day, which eventually led up to close to a bottle of tequila a day. I have no idea how I lived through that first year. I was so angry and hateful and had no idea how to work through what I was going through. I had no idea how to live and no idea how to die!

Three weeks after the assault in a drunk and not-okay state, I deleted my entire book on military PTSD. I realized that no matter how much rewriting of the story I had done, I had no idea how to live with the sensations I was having in my body. I felt defeated and helpless. The book was about three-fourths of the way done. It was missing the section on how to heal the sensations (emotional body). I didn't yet know how to do it. So in a moment of frustration and helplessness, I hit delete and deleted the trash also.

The bottom of my hole was pitch-black and covered in a tar-like substance. It had gotten too deep to climb the slippery walls, and I had zero desire to try anymore. I found comfort in the isolation, silence, and pain. At least this pain I knew, and it gave me reasons to not function and to hide. I truly just wanted anyone and everyone to leave me alone. If I could have naturally fallen asleep and never woken up, I would have.

But my bottom had a bottom. Four months after the assault, my oldest brother passed away. The pain, anger, rage, and devastation that went through me could never be explained in words. I wanted to peel my skin off and hang myself with my veins.

In my drunken, dead state, I remembered what Gavlin said to me: "April, I'm dead!" I thought, "I now know what that feels like."

CHAPTER 7

Facing Myself

❧

I LOOK BACK NOW AND realize I was kicking and screaming the whole way down. I partook in any outside distraction possible. Unaware that my thoughts were pulling me around as if I had a ring in my nose, I was completely lost in the torture chamber I had created. My emotional pain had become physically painful. If I could have climbed out of my skin, I would have. There was no escaping the aching, hurting, nightmares, insomnia, or flashbacks.

Over the years, I had done a lot of work on breaking down my story, changing my inner language, eating healthier, and exercising, but I had done little work on my emotional body. For a long time, I didn't even know it existed, and once I was aware, I had no idea how to access or release it.

I was so burned out and tired of trying to figure out a way to metamorphosize into who knows what to be okay. I was not accountable for the mold I was. I still had stories that I used to explain why I was how I was because of this or that. Yes, maybe there are so-called reasons the mold (me) was crafted as such, but I was now the one orchestrating the shape. It's hard to own that you are the one responsible. When I assumed the responsibility that I was creating the mold, I started to step more into my power. In accountability, there was power. In blame, I was powerless.

In that god-awful hole that I seemed to enjoy, where pain had become my safe friend, I knew I couldn't keep staying there. This was a slow death if I continued to be who I was being. I hated life! I hated myself! I thought, "I am a good person. I have tried very hard in life. I do not deserve this or what has happened to me." Deep in self-pity, blame, helplessness, hate, and rage, I was incredibly destructive. I had always been powerful at manifesting—someone who is angry, and throwing a tantrum equals a lot of destruction.

The first year I isolated and stayed drunk and/or stoned. I was trying to die. About a year after the sexual assault, I ran into Gavlin. Of course I was completely intoxicated. He told me he was in a relationship. I couldn't breathe.

I asked him if I was the love of his life. (Stupid drunk question!)

He said, "No!"

Shocked, I asked, "Do you have any regrets about her?"

I could see and feel the question had an emotional response within him. He answered, "Yes, she is married now!"

My whole world shattered. No, my story shattered. The pain consumed me, and I couldn't breathe. Gavlin had told me he loved me, but what became evident was that we had very different levels of love toward one another. In hindsight,

I still would have done everything I had done, but the story in my head put me through so much more than reality did.

My death mission intensified with my reckless disregard for my safety or life. The following two months are a blur. It was not seeing Gavlin that pushed me over the edge but what came up inside me. Without realizing it, I started to believe that everyone was better off without me: Gavlin, my son, Dennis, and my friends. My inner pain and torture were so great that people didn't want to be around me, and I didn't want to be around people or myself.

Then Gavlin came to see me. I have no idea what he wanted to tell me that night because in my drunken, angry state, I refused to talk to him. I ignored him for about an hour until he finally left. I was still in love with him. Nothing had changed for me emotionally, but I couldn't take any more pain. I knew because of the state I was in, he wouldn't be with me, and I wasn't able to be with him either. I wanted to die, and even being with him wasn't going to change that.

Finally, when I was at death's door, a dear friend said to me, "Either hurry up and die, or get busy living! Heal yourself or kill yourself because no one wants to watch you slowly kill yourself anymore." What she said was brilliant! No one had ever given me permission to just let go and not have to be here anymore. I always thought I had to do life. Now I had permission. Yay! Call it reverse psychology if you like, but it shifted something in me. I planned my exit strategy with excitement. The thought of dying and all my pain being gone was exciting. As I pondered this deep inside myself, I was haunted by a question: "Why can't I accomplish peace without death? Why do I have to give my life up just so I don't have to hurt anymore?"

I felt defeated after so many years of working on myself. I hated the universe (God, source, all that is). I felt betrayed. I had tried so hard to be okay and had spent my life helping other people heal. I felt abandoned, alone, and afraid. There was no one left but me. Because of my anger, I didn't want to ask the universe for help. Finally, in this very defeated, beyond-knowledge, helpless state, I did what I had always done: I looked to my intuition for answers. This time I wasn't doing it for a client. I was doing it for me, and a sense of determination bubbled up from deep inside me. I thought, "If anyone can figure out how to heal the emotional body, it's me!"

One night while incredibly intoxicated, I sat in my car in an empty parking lot screaming until I had no voice. During this process I remembered the Breath Release sessions I had done years prior. The sensation of a mass coming out of my throat had scared me, and I never went back. I realized I was no longer scared of Breath Release. What I was currently going through was far worse. I couldn't wait to go back and see if it helped.

As long as I live, I will never forget my first breath session upon returning. There were five other people there that night. During the session I had to go to the bathroom. I returned from the bathroom, and as I entered the room, I could see different colors of smog coming out of people— the same smog I had been seeing in cell tissue but couldn't access. It was moving up and out of them. I was stunned! I wanted to scream out loud and jump up and down, yelling, "How are you doing that? How are you doing that?" Of course I didn't, but that started the wheels turning in my head. I only went to a couple of sessions prior to being kicked out because I was too angry. The breath practitioner thought I needed more one on one, which she did not offer. I didn't have any money for private sessions, which left me out in the cold trying to heal on my own. In hindsight, this was perfect because the breath practitioner could never have healed me. I was the only one that could heal me. This forced me to hold my own hand and be with myself, even if I didn't like it.

I started that night in my car holding my guides' hands, determined and petrified. Night after night I would do a fast rhythm of breath, in through the nose and out through the mouth. I would go deep into an altered state, where I was still conscious. Sometimes I would walk back through experiences in my life, as the emotional body moved out of me; sometimes I would not. As the emotions separated from the cell tissue, it was painful at times. It felt like trying to separate Jell-O from water after it had dissolved. It was impossible to put into words everything that I had let go of. Most of it had no words (story) because it was emotions.

At this point, I was not able to describe what I was doing, but I knew it was helping. I felt calmer, and I was sleeping better. The breath sessions intimidated me. Many times I would pray for courage and strength to let go of the emotions and help me be strong enough to move it out of me.

MOVING MY EMOTIONAL BODY OUT

The first emotion I had to work through was resistance: "I don't want to do this." The first fifteen to twenty minutes of my breath sessions, I was kicking and screaming as I moved resistance out of me. I resisted almost everything: people, food, thoughts, emotions, situations, and life. Here is where I met the emotion of willing and unwilling. I decided to be willing, and that opened up a door for me to heal. If I had continued to be unwilling and resistant, I would still be stuck. Resistance came up in every session. How strong my resistance was depended on how much I didn't want to let go. I would see myself holding on to a symbolical rope. Sometimes in the impression, I could see my hands bleeding, I was holding on so tight. The process of letting go can feel very scary and unknown. I mustered up courage within me and begged my guides for strength and support, because I knew I had to keep going and letting go, even if it was hard.

During a session, I decided one night to use Breath Release to revisit the conversation I had had with my dad in the shed. (I told this story at the beginning of the book.) I had done years of inner child work and had done years of rewriting the story, but I was unable to let go of what happened. So much healing over the years had come from this event, yet there was a part of me still hooked because I could see myself there. A very faint fuzzy me, but I was still there. That night in Breath Release, I saw that my dad's pride was what caused him to say the things he had and act the way he did to me that day. I burst into tears. As I was breathing the sensations out of me, I could see the same tendencies in me. I was prideful. Pride had resulted in me ending friendships, walking away from jobs, hurting people's feelings, needing to be right, being above people, hurting my son and Dennis, hurting myself, isolating myself from others, and so much more. As I looked at my relationship with pride and how I used pride, my heart hurt so deeply. I could see what it was creating in my life. It was very painful and life changing to look at how I used pride as a shield to protect me from being close to people. I could see so much fear and defensive reacting because of my dance with pride over the years. This was the start of me shifting my relationship with pride. Years of emotional pain due to how I played with pride released out of my cell tissue.

Sometimes, as I moved the emotional history out of my body, it felt like it was burning. I remember hearing in my head, "It's like standing in the fire as it burns through you." This sensation was very strong within in me as I released discontent, condescending, thinking "I'm better or smarter" or "I'm above you, and I'm right." Years of conversation ran through me. Without realizing it, I talked to people in a condescending, sarcastic way as if they were stupid. If they were stupid, then I must be right, and then they will listen to me, *right?* I did this unknowingly with so many people: friends, employees, and people I didn't even know. I was prideful in needing to be right. This gave me some kind of false power at the expense of others. For me to be above, special, or important, it meant you needed to be lower or less than me.

When I woke up to how I was doing this and how much I did it, I couldn't breathe. Each breath felt like fire burning through my chest, esophagus, and throat. Once I realized I had treated people I loved this way, the anger I had toward myself was indescribable. I treated others this way out of fear. I had a false belief if they needed me in some way—my wisdom, my caring, my spiritual knowledge, my experience, or my intuition—then they wouldn't walk away from me. In looking at why I needed people to need me, I realized it created a false sense of safety within me. This process was not easy but liberating. The truth is people do not need me, and I do not need them to need me. Relationships that are built on a foundation of need depend on one of the parties being strong and one of the parties to be weak. This is a very scary thought because someone can die, decide not to have you in his or her life, or the relationship could change in some way. Trying to keep or force someone to stay in your life through need creates resentment and power struggles. You need the other person to be submissive in order for them to need you. Most people do not like being or staying in a submissive position just to make you feel better.

On another occasion, I was trying to move hurt out of my chest. My chest hurt so deeply that it was hard to breathe. I was revisiting different events in my childhood when my parents unknowingly taught me to hurt myself. They hurt themselves all the time. Even cutting me out of their lives was an act of self-hurt, but they honored their beliefs over what was right for them. I was shown thousands of examples of self-punishment: how I talked to myself and made myself constantly do things that hurt me. I remember in the middle of the session screaming out, "I don't want to hurt me anymore!" I kept screaming it over and over again as years of emotional self-mutilation poured out of me, years of whipping myself emotionally. The things I had done that hurt me—to get a man's love, to pay the bills, to be accepted by peers and friends, to be important, to be heard, to belong, to be wanted, or to be enough. I was hurting myself, and I didn't want to do it anymore. I have to say this was one of the biggest releases that created me being a much different person with others and myself. Years of hurt came out of my body. Also, when I analyzed my relationship with hurt, I noticed I wanted to make someone pay, and I would make myself pay by hurting myself. This is why I drank, had eating disorders, and had so many other self-punishing behaviors.

I even released happiness, joy, love, and excitement out of my cell tissue. Growing up, I constantly got in trouble because I was too excited and hyper. My whole life, I managed my excitement. At times, I suppressed my happiness over accomplishments so other people wouldn't feel bad or because I believed I didn't deserve it. I blocked years of love toward my son and others out of fear of loss and control.

Releasing the energy of deserving out of my body was hard. My mind really wanted to get in the way and tell me I deserved or didn't deserve. This led to emotions like self-punishment, guilt, and feeling bad or unworthy.

Not being wanted was another huge emotional release for me. I had lots of stories in my head that told me I was unwanted, but the truth was that I didn't want me. I didn't want my body. I didn't want my thoughts. I didn't want my life. I didn't want anything about me. Tears rained out of me as I screamed, "I want me! I want me!"

Anger and rage came out of the body in growling sounds. I was so angry with myself for all the emotional self-mutilation. I had so much rage over decisions that I had made or not made. Up until this point, I really struggled with chest colds and bronchitis. For months, I would cough, and it sounded like I was barking at the world. I have never had bronchitis again and very rarely get chest colds. Along with the emotional changes, it was shocking how many physical changes were happening.

When I was working through abandonment, I decided to stop drinking and smoking weed. I didn't stop overnight, but this emotional release made me want to. My story was filled with abandonment, but the truth was that I was abandoning myself. I wanted to check out of my life constantly and loved being checked out. I abandoned my life all the time. In Breath Release I promised to start showing up in life for me. Not because I had to, but because I loved myself and wanted to.

When I was moving fear and being petrified out of my cell tissue, I almost gave up. At first, as you breathe into the cell tissue to move the emotion, it intensifies. It got so intense and painful that I actually got to a point that I could not breathe. I was so deep in years of fear that it took my breath away. I remember thinking, "I love me! I love me!" trying to get myself through it. Alone and determined, I purged years of petrifying fear out of me.

Loss! I remember the night I moved loss through me. I had experienced so much loss that I was lost in it. I had lost myself in work, relationships, addictions, emotions, and thoughts. Loss of yourself being present is devastating. I didn't know who I was for years. Connecting to myself deep inside healed, as I released years of loss out of me.

I released devastation, disgust, stubborn, value, embarrassment, shame, guilt, pleasure, regret, betrayal, violation, aloneness, lost, isolation, anguish, ecstasy, sorrow, gratitude, mourning, lacking, badness, unlovable feelings, and hundreds more emotions out of my cell tissue. Night after night, the screaming, growling, and coughing created space within me. The space felt like calmness and serenity. Years of emotional pain that had become physical pain poured out of me.

In the thralls of a release one night, crying, alone, and scared, I made a promise to people that are suffering: "If I make it through this, I promise I will create safe places to heal energies such as rage, violation, anger, helplessness, unfairness, and so on! I promise if you help me heal, I will help others!"

In the beginning, I was scared of the pain coming back. There was an obvious difference in my body. I felt calmer and more peaceful. There was stillness in my body that I had never felt, and I held my excitement back, afraid that the sensations would come back. But they did not! I still had emotions in the moment and still struggled with suppressing, blocking, and cutting off behavior, but the years of history I moved out of my cell tissue was just gone. Finally, I could breathe deeper, I could sleep, and I started to feel safe. I had so much space inside me. It felt amazing.

I was starting to understand the emotional body more and more as I worked with it. I noticed that all of the emotions in my body did not belong to someone else. This meant that I did not take on other people's anger, hate, or rage and have to release it. No—these were my emotions that I had suppressed, blocked, or cut off. It was me that created these emotions stuck within my cell tissue.

You cannot learn to flow. Flow is what your body naturally does with emotions until we are taught suppression as children. Think about a baby who has not learned to block emotions yet. If a baby feels an emotion, he or she responds with no filter. Again, you cannot learn to flow because you already know how to do that, but you can discover why you block, suppress, and cut off the emotions. Once you stop doing things that block the flow of emotions, they naturally flow again.

I started to notice different thoughts I believed that stopped the flow of emotions. I believed emotions like anger were negative or bad, so I suppressed them. I was afraid of their power and didn't want to experience them. This is why your relationship with every energy is important. The energies that I had a bad relationship with all ended up stuck in my body. I had to change the relationship and then move the old emotional history out.

I was starting to heal, but further healing and focusing on me was still my main goal. Unfortunately, healing yourself does not pay the bills. I didn't want to be around people just yet, but I wanted to do readings. This led me to psychic phone readings. I had so many mixed emotions going into this experience, but what I can tell you is I learned so much. Wow, did I learn a lot about humans and how we work, function, and create.

CHAPTER 8

Phone Readings

❧

I HAD ONLY EXPERIENCED DOING readings with Dr. Karen and clients on health-related issues and healing. I had never put myself out there as a psychic. I anticipated more personal questions about love and money, but I really didn't know what I was signing up for. What I found out was that psychic readings are harder than reading for doctors.

When you tell people something they don't want to hear, they can get very upset. This is not always fun to deal with. When a person is trying to heal from an ailment, he or she is more open to hearing things the person doesn't want to hear in order to heal.

Even though I didn't realize why, throughout my life I would upset people with the things that I would say. For me, it was just a truth that I was pointing out while making an observation. In relationships, I would experience people holding me on a pedestal and raving about me until I pointed at stories they believed were their absolute truths. It was as though I had committed an act of murder, which caused them to try and discredit me. If I am wrong, then they can hold onto their story. Sometimes I can feel a wedge between us, as though the distance or space will negate the truth.

They could also be judging themselves for what I see. If you are embarrassed about certain aspects of yourself, then the sensation of being seen will make you want to hide. If this happens within a person because of something I have pointed at, then he or she starts to avoid me. It changes the person's view of me. I struggle with this emotionally. I have said to friends, "So you love your story about me more than me?" I can't tell you how many female friends I've lost because I didn't tell them what they wanted to hear about some man of interest when they have asked me! I'm not talking about me shoving information down someone's throat; they asked me. This is why I will not read for my friends anymore. Also, because this is what I do for a living, I don't want to do it all the time. If one of your friends is a general contractor, I'm sure you do not expect this person to constantly work on your house. I'm no different. I don't want to read for people constantly, especially because it sometimes affects the friendship.

When I'm getting intuitive hits, they are unemotional for me. It's like I'm watching a movie, and I'm telling you about it. This does not mean I do not understand the electrical shocks that go through the body when someone points at my story. (This happens because of attachment to the story and because of self-judgment.)

PHONE READINGS

Phone readings are not sessions. They are two- to five-minute conversations where the caller tries to ask as many questions as possible as fast as possible. They want accurate, fast answers. They want to know outcomes and the complicated multilayers of a situation or person in two minutes.

I have been more verbally beaten up doing phone readings then I ever experienced as a medical intuitive. This also reflects how strong our attachment is to what we want. Unfortunately, most current online platforms for this kind of service are disrespectful to how sacred intuition is. They allow individuals to rate the readers. In the business world, this may make sense, but in the spiritual world it is offensive. If an angel or passed-over loved one appeared before you and told you something, would you rate him or her? So either the platform does not believe it has readers of this magnitude, or they are being disrespectful. I do believe that my history of holding my intuition as sacred is another reason I'm strongly connected to it.

People assume feedback and ratings have to do with reading accuracy, but in truth it has more to do with whether a client is feeling good after the call. This encourages readers to lie or be dishonest as they make more money and do not receive as much negative feedback. This is not the way I roll. It is not my responsibility or business if you are happy. My ad does not say, "Call for happiness!" This may sound cold, but in the long run, from my experience, the truth is the most beneficial for people. I'm not selling happiness! I'm offering my intuition to you, which means I focus on describing what I see, hear, and feel as accurately as possible without an agenda to make you happy or feel any other emotion. I do hold my intuition as sacred, and I try very hard to not disgrace it by being intimidated. It does you no good if I lie to you or encourage your story.

After two months of having tomatoes thrown at me, I was done. I was still healing and had no idea what to do for money. It took a couple months of meditation and self-reflecting to figure out what phone readings were bringing up within me. I had to let go of what I was not responsible for or what was not my business. It is not my business if a person doesn't like what I'm saying. It is not my business if a person listens to me or believes me. It is my business to provide an honest and clear reading. I do not need to be nasty or nice. I need to be honest. If the person doesn't like the reading, then don't use my intuition. I recommend that everyone develop his or her own intuition. This helped me create an internal foundation so I could do phone readings successfully. I do not sugarcoat! I tell you what I see and give you space to react any way you want. You can be angry, unhappy, or hurt. I'm okay with emotions, but when someone directs anger at me, of course I'm going to protect myself and my business and not continue to read for him or her.

Eventually I tried with my new inner foundation to provide phone readings again. It took several months, but I built a large base of customers. My feedback started to reflect that I was an honest reader with regular comments. I would hear constantly, "Oh, other readers have been saying for months (sometimes years) he loves me!" After being told what you want to hear for a while and having it not come true, people get angry. Finally, they just want the truth, even if they do not like it because waiting and holding on to false hope is very painful. I will not do this to anyone. The courage it takes to be honest is tremendous.

My intuition is meant for me. What is right for me may not be right for you. This is why it's more important for me to teach intuition than to do readings. It's like trying to be powerful for someone else, think for someone else, feel for someone else, or let something go for someone else. There are many things in life only each person can do for himself or herself. Intuition is designed for each person. I do not believe I have the answers for you. I can tell you what I see or what I would do, but you are the only one who knows your truth!

Very quickly I noticed during phone readings, I was saying the same things over and over again. Phone readings helped me see thousands of different ways we allow our stories to control us. It's like we are all under a spell until we let go of the story and wake up. I say "all" because this statement includes me. I have stories. I'm still woven into time just like everyone else. Just because I can see the waves of time and how we are creating, doesn't mean I have mastered letting go of everything. I share what I see, but I do not mislead people to believe I have it all figured out or mastered. It's not my responsibility to be anyone's opinion of perfect. It is my responsibility to be honest.

LIFE IS NOT SET IN STONE

Life is not set in stone or black and white. For example, if someone asks me, "When am I going to get married?" I respond with something like this: Your life is not that written in stone. It's not like on December 6, you are going to get married. What I read is based on your current energy and what you will most likely create. I can tell you most likely what is going to happen based on different components like thoughts believed, experiences in life, and your relationship with emotions. Most answers are not black and white. People can get mad at this or think I'm not really psychic. Think about this: If I told you that your life is written in stone and you have no choice, how would you feel about that? At times, I do see a clear black-and-white answer, but most of the time, I see options and percentages. I can tell you in detail what a person is like, why they are doing what they are doing, and what they will most likely do. I can also tell you if you make different decisions how each decision would most likely play out.

People minimize how complex of beings we are. We are brilliant, multidimensional beings, and we minimize ourselves down to believing there is a simple single answer to a situation or person. The layering of a person's programming is one of the hardest and most complicated puzzles you will ever see.

LOVE AND RELATIONSHIPS

Usually when it comes to romantic love, people will ask me, "Are they interested in me, or do they love me?" People usually ask this question because they believe that if a person is interested or loves them, that equals a relationship, but it doesn't. That couldn't be any further from the truth.

First, there are several different ways we can feel attraction or connect with someone.

Mind connection. You and the other person have similar beliefs about life, and you feel very mentally stimulated by this person during conversations. If I'm reading a practical person, he or she will have a list of what the person wants in a mate. If I see this, I will usually say something like, "On paper you fit what they are looking for."

Physical connection. You and the other person have a very strong sexual connection. A sense of craving and longing for the other person will be intense. Wanting to be close to this person even if you're not having sex will also feel very satisfying.

Emotional connection. You emotionally respond to this person. This person could make you feel nervous, warm and fuzzy inside, giddy, and young. (Someone's heart and chest warmth toward another person will have lots of beautiful colors coming out of them and going into the other person.)

Spiritual connection. You will say things like, "I can't explain it, but I feel like I've always known them" or "I've always loved them." This connection is always laced with a sense you cannot explain or understand. You just know it's there.

Having any or all of the above connections does not constitute a relationship. What determines a relationship?

Capacity. Does this person have the capacity to create a relationship? This person may not have any time or energy remaining. He or she may already be creating so much in life that there is no room for a relationship, or the person is unwilling or can't change that. Capacity also can mean mental or emotional limitations. If a person is struggling with PTSD or addictions, he or she will not have the mental or emotional capacity to sustain a consistent relationship.

Relationship. A person's relationship with love is crucial in determining whether there is relationship potential. For some people, when love is in their bodies, it makes them want to run for the hills. They prefer superficial relationships to being deeply in love. Some people are obsessed with love. They can't get enough of it and want to roll in it all the time. Some people can take it or leave it. Then there are people who are very structured with their love. They will decide how much love to give different people in their lives based on a practical decision they believe is right for them. There are thousands of different relationships a person can have with the energy of love. A person's relationship with love will determine whether he or she will have a relationship with someone or not. It will also determine the kind of relationship this person will have.

Level. You can connect with someone in several different ways, but the level of love each of you want or need could be very different. I end up saying, "I don't think the issue is going to be your connection, but the level you want to experience and share love is very different then the level within the person you are asking about. You will have to decide if this is enough for you."

Story. The stories that each person carries about love is huge and different from person to person. I hear all the time, "Well if they loved me..." A person's perception on what love is or how to love will not be someone else's. I usually end up saying something like, "I do see love in them toward you, but they do not have the same views on love that you do."

Timing. If it is not the right time in a person life for a relationship, it is simply not the right time. This can be due to financial issues, a divorce, someone dying, children, emotional issues, or someone going through spiritual growth. Trying to change or force timing is like trying to make a meat thermometer in a turkey pop before it's cooked. You just can't force it. It's done when it's done. Timing is right when it's right.

Compatibility. Look at the list above of different ways to connect with someone. Compatibility increases the more connections you have with a person. If you only have a sexual connection with someone, regardless of how amazing the sex is, this does not equal a long-term relationship. If you have the most amazing, stimulating conversations ever with someone, that still does not equal a relationship. The more connections you have with someone, the stronger your compatibility will be.

Personality. You can be connected to someone in every way, and if the person has horrible personality traits or addictions, you will not have a healthy relationship. It takes time to really know a person. I have said many times, "You're asking me if this person likes you, but you don't know how they are when they're mad, how are they when they are angry or hurt. Are they selfish, loving, and giving? There are about a hundred things to discover about someone before it's important to know if they are interested in you."

Needs. Love is not the only reason a person wants to be in a relationship. Sometimes other energies are more important. This may be an unconscious motive to the person. People may say they want to be in love, but what they truly want is safety, a sense of belonging, home, to be accepted, someone to take care of them, or a mate so they don't have to be alone.

I am constantly learning from readings. In the following stories, all of the names have been changed (and sometimes gender) to protect the privacy of the individuals.

LOVE
<u>Caller 1</u>

CALLER 1: I want to know if Mark, forty-two, is going to step it up in our relationship.'

APRIL: Show me Mark, forty-two! Show me Mark, forty-two! *(I ask for the person's first name and age in order to read them, and then I ask for them to energetically come forward.)* Okay, Mark is standing in front of me. He is a very nice guy. I can see why you like him, but what I don't see here is a lot of effort. This guy comes across to me like he goes with the flow. Easy come, easy go. If it's meant to stay, it will stay.

Unfortunately, because of this, I don't see him putting a lot of effort into this relationship. He is way too lackadaisical to create what I would call a relationship! I do not think this is the level of relationship you want.

CALLER 1: Will that change?

APRIL: This guy is who he is. He is satisfied and content. I do not see a desire in him to be different. When I scroll out into time eight to ten months ahead, he still feels like the same person to me with minimal change.

CALLER 1: Is there anything I can do to change that?

APRIL: No, I don't intuitively see that you can change him. Plus I'm hearing from a guide, "Do you love this man as he is or after the remodeling job?" Who he is as a person right now is not who you love. You want him to be different. I don't see a strong enough desire in him to be different. So as he is right now with no change, do you want to be with him?

CALLER 1: No! So he doesn't love me enough to work on this?

APRIL: I see he loves you, but he is who he is. If you want a man that is going to show up and truly be a mate, plan life with you, be consistent, and eventually marry you, this is not the guy you asked me about. You would need to go find someone like that.

CALLER 1: So then this is just over?

APRIL: No, I didn't say it was over. I continue to see this guy in your energy field over the next several months, but he is not offering a deep, committed, and consistent relationship. If you want that, then this is not your guy.

Waiting and hoping for a person to be different is not fun and is usually painful. If there are things about a person that need to change in order for you to have a relationship with him or her, then ask the person if he or she wants to change. I wouldn't recommend hoping that they do or trying to force them into it with manipulation. There is a difference between two people growing together and one person trying to change the other person when there is no interest in changing.

CALLER 2

CALLER 2: There is a girl named Shelly, twenty-four. We use to date, but she broke up with me. She has been hanging around her ex but sending me pictures of her. She tells me she is not interested, but then why is she sending me pictures of her with her kid?

APRIL: Show me Shelly, twenty-four! Show me Shelly, twenty-four! I see a safety net. She definitely doesn't want to lose you out of her energy field, but I see it's for safety reasons, not because of love. She actually does have love coming out of her toward the other guy you mentioned, but he will never be with her. He strings her along but will never be with her. I would believe the words that she is telling you.

CALLER 2: Okay, then why is she sending me pictures and texting me?

APRIL: I understand that you want the texting and pictures to mean she wants to be with you, but one does not equal the other. I do not see her showing up and being in a constant relationship with you. In fact, I would be careful with her because she is hanging on to you for the sensation of safety, and that confuses you and keeps you hooked.

A person's intention is very important, and unfortunately most people are not aware of what their true motives are or where they are coming from. When you are hopeful in a situation, you will take any little bread crumb and try to turn it into a loaf of bread. I hear often, "So they're just using me?" Most of the time I do not read in people that they are consciously using other people. Getting our needs for safety, attention, nurturing, important, and belonging met is usually an unconscious driver within us that takes deep reflection and self-honesty to uncover. It is not until a situation is over that we can look back and see more clearly the dynamics being played out by both parties.

CALLER 3

CALLER 3: I want you to read a guy named Gary, fifty-six. I've had several other readers tell me he is my twin flame, and I want to know when you see us meeting?

APRIL: Show me Gary, fifty-six! Show me Gary, fifty-six! Okay, a man comes across that has his back to me, but he is turned just a little so I can see the side of his shoulder partially. He isn't really giving me his attention, but because he is partially turned, as if you are in his peripheral vision, he is aware of you but not really doing anything. I don't see him heading toward you. When I'm in his mind, I do not see many thoughts about you. I see him looking to the future and has fun things planned that he wants to do. He feels busy and social to me, but what I'm not seeing is him putting any effort into meeting you or building a relationship.

CALLER 3: Okay, I want to ask about someone else. *(The caller went on to ask about another guy.)*

I do not use terms like "soul mate" or "twin flame." These labels confuse people. Let's just say that if these terms actually exist, it doesn't matter. What does matter is whether the person shows up in your life and what kind of a person he or she is. Would the person make a loving, kind, and considerate mate, and does he or she want a relationship? You can call someone whatever title you want, but that does not equal a relationship. I've had people call me and say they are in a relationship, but when I read the situation, it feels nothing like a relationship. I describe my impressions and try not to label situations.

CALLER 4

CALLER 4: When is he going to leave his wife?

APRIL: I don't see him leaving. He is unhappy and dissatisfied, but I don't see him leaving. He would have to give up more than he is willing to give up. I see her (his wife) leaving before he does. She feels fed up to me and about to walk.

CALLER 4: When do you see her leaving?

APRIL: I can't answer that. If she honored how she feels, she would have already left, but her fears and obligations keep her hanging on. It's impossible to know for sure how long she will be able to go against her truth. My best guesstimate is eight to ten months more. I can see some planning going on within her thoughts about an exit strategy, but I do not see any actions yet.

CALLER 4: Does he love me?

APRIL: He loves what he doesn't want to give up more, or he would have already left. I see caring in his heart toward you, a very strong sexual connection, but I wouldn't call what I'm looking at love. When I'm in this man's thoughts, I hear more thoughts about himself then thoughts about other people."

CALLER 4: Do you see us together eventually?

APRIL: No! I see you getting angry with him because even after he and his wife separate, he will not do what you want him to. I see him dating other women for about eighteen months to two years before settling back into a relationship. I see you being mad and angry. I don't see him closing this gap between the two of you. I'm sorry!

CALLER 4: Will someone new come into my life?

APRIL: Eventually, but you are greatly affecting the timing on meeting someone new because you are holding onto the other guy you just asked me about. I think this is going to be a process for you to let go and open up to someone new. I see several stepping-stones across a pond. What that tells me is you will date several different guys prior to settling down. Each stepping-stone (guy) will help you heal in a different way, and some of the guys will even open you up to new experiences. Try to enjoy this process.

Timing is greatly affected by free will. There is no way to determine how long someone will suffer. Some people get intuitive hits, and they move very quickly, but others stay stuck a long time. This is not good or bad but a choice. Each choice has a different experience and a different cause and effect. I've heard many times, "I know this is going to hurt like hell, but I'm going to do it anyway!" Sometimes we just want to touch the hot pot. There are people who only want to learn from experiencing things, while others are satisfied with the mind knowledge of the experience. This will also change depending on the experience. Some people will sign up for hurt in romantic relationship but would never do jobs they hate. Each person, depending on the programming and energetic makeup, will be different.

MONEY

Money has become an energy because the entire human race has given it power. It is no different than any other energy; you will have a relationship with it. Even if you didn't realize it, you will have thoughts and emotions about money. Possible thoughts could be as follows: "Money is the source of all evil"; "Easy come, easy go"; "Money isn't a big deal to me"; "Everything I touch turns to gold"; "Live within your means"; and lots more. Your relationship with other energies will have an influence on your relationship with money. Energies that I've witnessed that have an impact are deservedness, lack, not enough, scarcity, practicality, loss, power, control, emptiness, shame, guilt, and badness.

CALLER 5

CALLER 5: How do you see my finances going this year?

APRIL: Up and down is the impression. It's not that money isn't flowing in, but you live within your means, so the minute you have money, regardless of how much, you will spend it. You are the kind of person that always makes ends meet but never has extra money because extra money to you means fun, clothes, and other things that you want. This is not good or bad, but if you want money in your savings account, then you will have to change your relationship with money. You have to value saving it more than the things you want to spend it on. You do not have to do this, but what is needed if you want to save money.

CALLER 5: You're right! So do you ever see me buying a house?

APRIL: I see the opportunity dropping into your energy field in about eight to ten months. I see an older man in your life that will help you with the down payment, possibly a father figure or your father.

CALLER 5: My grandfather? He raised me!

APRIL: That feels right when you say it. He will help you when the time is right.

It's not uncommon for people to spend what they have. When you have no money, you can make twenty bucks last forever. When you have hundreds of dollars, it flows right through your hand. This creates a pattern. At times I will say to someone, "Learn to control you!" You may not always be able to control the money flow toward you, but you can control how you spend it.

CALLER 6

CALLER 6: I've been visualizing lots of money coming into my life. When do you see this happening?

APRIL: I get the impression of a car, and you are sitting outside of the car on the ground, but you are not driving anywhere. Visualizations alone without actions mean nothing. I do not get a timeframe because there is not enough energy being weaved into this to create it. Right now, it is just a thought in your head. Action is needed to birth it.

Energy flow into a situation or idea can tell me timing on when it will manifest. I say this a lot, regardless of what the person is trying to create. You're just thinking about it; call me back when you decide to invest more energy into it, and then I can give you a timeframe.

The car visual I mentioned about I see have seen in different ways, in different readings. Where the person is in the car symbolically tells me how he or she approaches decision making and creating in life.

1. When the person is in the driver's seat, this person is very driven and is going somewhere, even if he or she doesn't know where.

2. When the person is in the passenger seat, this person wants other people to drive his or her life. This person will look to other people to say what decisions are right for this person and what to do with his or her life.

3. When the person is in the back seat, I will actually hear "back-seat driver." This person will not listen to others or himself or herself about life but will try to tell everyone around how to drive (live).

4. The impression above, in which the client is actually outside the car, was the first time I saw this impression. It took me several minutes to figure out what I was being shown. Finally, I realized that this person is going nowhere and doing nothing. The person is just lost in what is called "visualizing," but no driving or movement is happening.

CALLER 7

CALLER 7: Do you see any money coming my way?

APRIL: No. I get the impression of you looking up at the sky with your hand out. No, I do not see money just falling in your lap. I do not see you winning the lotto or a rich family member dying. You are capable and need to take care of yourself. You are worth working for. You are worth the work. Go provide for you.

When it comes to money, a lot of people have a parent/child relationship with it. It makes them mad when they have to ask for it and when they have to provide for themselves. You are not a child, and there is no parent who is going to take care of you in life. Change your relationship with money, and master it. Money is a tool. You have a say in how to use it. Learn how to use this tool.

CALLER 8

CALLER 8: Do you see me being okay financially?

APRIL: I'm not sure what you mean. When I look at you, I see money all around you. You feel more than okay when it comes to money.

CALLER 8: Well, I'm going through a divorce, and he isn't wanting to give me what I deserve. Is he going to?

APRIL: Your question is not are you going to be okay! Your question is, am I going to get what I want, and how much?

CALLER 8: Yes, that is what I want to know.

APRIL: I see a 40/60 split. You get the 40.

CALLER 8: So I don't get half of everything?

APRIL: It feels close to me, but I see he had things prior to the marriage, and I see him keeping that.

CALLER 8: Okay, that's true.

I've found when reading for people about money that what one person thinks is nothing is another person's pot of gold. A person's relationship with the energy of enough affects the experience with money. For some people, it will never be enough. They could stockpile money and still want more.

As you dive into your relationship with money and why you are creating it or not creating it, you will be surprised at what affects it and what doesn't. I can't give you every possible scenario with money. Part of the joy of mastering energies is figuring out how you play with them and what they are creating in your life.

WEIGHT LOSS OR GAIN
Caller 9

CALLER 9: I'm trying to lose fifteen pounds before my sister's wedding. Do you see that happening?

APRIL: No, I actually don't see that. It's not that you can't, but your relationship with food would have to be changed. I see a woman sitting gobbling up everything in front of her. This is the only area in your life that isn't controlled. I see from childhood extreme control around you. The *only* area I see where you believe you have freedom is to eat. I do not see you giving this up until you have freedom in other areas of your life. This is also why it's so hard for you, because most people do not want to give up a source of happiness, especially when it's one of their only sources.

We gobble up food as joy, happiness, and life. Food is symbolic of life. When you are not living in life, you will have a very strong urge to live through food. It can feel uncontrollable. To heal, this person would need to break down the walls of structure and control that keeps him or her from living. This is not an easy process because the person will have hundreds of reasons not to live.

CALLER 10

CALLER 10: I can't seem to lose weight, no matter how hard I try!

APRIL: I see padding here, meaning emotional protection. How do you talk to yourself within your mind? Do you beat yourself up constantly? Are you never good enough, always doing it wrong? Are you on yourself about every little thing: what to say, what not to say, how to be, how not to be, and so on!

CALLER 10: I guess.

APRIL: Stop emotionally beating yourself up, because your body is naturally protecting itself from you!

I see this a lot when it comes to weight gain. Physical or emotional abuse will create the body protecting itself in the only way it knows. If you were spanked a lot as a child on the outer thighs or butt, you will carry extra weight in these areas.

Every thought hits a different part of the body. If you gain weight in your stomach area, this is protection in the area of peers and social situations. It could be because when you are around people, you are very hard on yourself or because you feel that the people you are around are very hard on you. One feeds the other. I call this "safety weight."

CALLER 11

CALLER 11: What is it that I'm eating that creates my bloating?

APRIL: I don't see it's what you are eating but that you have a lot of anxiety in your body. The anxiety is creating acid and bloating. Some foods neutralize the acid and help, but the food is not the cause.

CALLER 11: I don't feel anxious.

APRIL: You feel anxious about what you eat or don't eat. You feel anxious about how things are going to turn out. You feel anxious if you are going to get it all done. You feel anxious about money and having enough. You are anxious about how people view you. Are you sure you're not anxious?

CALLER 11: *(laughs)*: Okay, maybe I am anxious. So when it comes to food, how do I know what to eat?

APRIL: Ask your body! Your body will always tell you what you are hungry for and how much you need, if you ask intuitively. You just have to ask and then listen.

This is incredibly important, regardless of what size you are. We are not taught that our body knows what it needs. Science has proven over and over again that we crave what we are lacking in nourishment naturally. Your knowledge gets in the way, telling you all the latest diets and opinions, but in truth you already have the perfect database within you if you ask. It will not only tell you what nourishment you need, but it will also tell you how much. The same goes for exercise. When you hear your body, you know how much movement it needs to stay fit and healthy. Again you have to listen to the perfect source for you, which is yourself.

CALLER 12

CALLER 12: Lately I've been really gaining weight. What is going on with me?

APRIL: Do you feel stuck in life?

CALLER 12: Yes! I went through a divorce four years ago, and I can't seem to get out of this funk.

APRIL: You are scared and not moving. Weight gain within you feels like creative energy stuck in the body. Part of the weight gain is safety, because you feel unsafe to me. You need to work through your fears of getting hurt, failing, and not being good enough so you can actively create again. Once you do that, the weight will fall off you.

A lot of extreme weight gain is creativity stuck in the body coupled with safety issues. This is the perfect soil to manifest lots of weight. It's a process to break down this pattern, especially if you learned this as a child. Childhood programming is usually a lot harder to change then habits learned as an adult. Be gentle with yourself as you create a safe place for your physical body and emotional body.

This chapter could be an entire book. I have learned so much from doing phone readings. What became very clear, over and over again, is the power that a person's story has over what he or she creates, how long it takes to create something, the effects on the person's health, and his or her life experiences.

Slowly I was doing better and better. Breath Release was changing the sensations in my body. The more I freed myself from my emotional history, the more I wanted to reengage in life. I knew my intuition had gotten a lot stronger, but I had not been engaging with people other than through phone readings. I was curious to see how much stronger my intuition had grown. Slowly, I started to emerge from my cocoon where I had been healing for over a year. It was time to see how the new me would do in the outside world.

CHAPTER 9

Maintaining

❦

IT WAS EASY TO MAINTAIN my new inner stillness when I was separate from everyone, but I also wanted to engage in life again. I was very different as a person after letting go of the mental and emotional history in my psyche and cell tissue. I was by no means free completely of the illusion of time, but I had let go enough to experience peace and stillness within me, and I didn't want to give that precious space up as I reentered into life.

Part of emerging successfully took me being honest and okay with myself about being human. It was never my goal to be just one frequency, such as love or peace. I do not consider an enlightened state to be an act of maintaining only one frequency when I am all frequencies. My goal was to have a good relationship with all aspects of me, which means all energies. I knew this was not going to be easy in a world where everyone has labeled more than half of us—half of the energies we are—as negative, bad, or lower frequencies. Be love, and do not feel hate! Be compassionate, and don't feel irritated or annoyed. Be kind; don't be angry. Act happy all the time, even when you're so stressed you can hardly breathe. It is not that people are not experiencing all frequencies (emotions), but we have been taught to put on a face and pretend to be acceptable energies to the people around us and hide or lie about the energies we have deemed as negative. That was a challenge for me as I reentered into society. I knew and understood the damage of suppressing, blocking, and rejecting, so I was not too keen on having to do it just to be around people.

When I was healing myself, I struggled with the fact that there was no space in our society for people to heal hard emotions like rage, anger, frustration, helplessness, and so on. We numb the emotions or talk about them without showing them, but we do not have safe places to release the emotions out of us. There is no space for people to feel the way they feel. If someone in a group is upset or angry, most of the time, everyone around the person will label him or her as negative. This encourages suppression in others and us.

I knew there were going to be times that other people's emotions would upset or scare me as I engaged with people. I decided to start intuitively asking things like, "Am I really in danger, or do I need to work on my relationship with the energy the person is exhibiting?" Ninety-nine percent of the time, I am *not* in danger; I'm just uncomfortable with the energy in front of me. Someone is just reflected a part of me that I am still uncomfortable with, and I need to cultivate a better relationship with that aspect of myself. When I am okay with me, I am okay with you. When I ask intuitively if I am in danger, I can feel that and decide to move away from the situation. There is a huge difference between truly being in danger and judging people for their emotions. My mind cannot figure out if I'm in danger or if I'm uncomfortable with the energy; however, my intuition can tell me right away.

I also noticed when I do not have a good relationship with an energy, I become selfish. I need people around me to be a certain way. In order for me to be okay, I need you to only be the frequencies of love, happiness, and positivity. I realized that I was very selfish to need other people to be a certain way in order for me to feel okay or to be around them. It was silly to give other people that much power over my state of being. It takes a very powerful person to maintain their energy while allowing other people the space to feel and be how they want. When I have a good relationship with all energies, this is easier for me to maintain and allow others space to be how they choose. If someone irks me, then I know I still have work to do there. It is me that has a problem with an energy, not the person who is using it. They are not my business; I am my business!

There are times I will move away from an energy even if I am safe—not because I think it is bad, but because it gets old. Just like it would get old to eat twenty pounds of fish, energies can get old. I'm tired of the arguing or debating— again, not because it's wrong or because I'm above you, but because my system has had enough of those frequencies for the moment. Then I move away from it without a story of it being bad or think, "How dare they!" If I hold on to any story about the situation, then I'm holding myself captive to it and not allowing myself to be free.

I do not need to fix you, save you, change you, enlighten you, or need you to need me. You are right where you need to be, and so am I. I do not need you to think certain thoughts or not think other thoughts to be around you. I do not need you to feel certain emotions but not feel other emotions. Just like I want the space to think and feel in a way that is right for me, I have to give others that same kind of space. As I became okay with where other people were with emotions and thoughts, the more I became okay with where I was.

I remind myself constantly that I will *never* run out of things to discover about myself or develop within myself, so there is no reason for me to wander outside of myself into other people's business. Of course this is what I do for a living, but if a person is not paying me money to read them, then that is not what our relationship is and not my business. No, I am not being loving or helpful. It doesn't love a person to want them to be different or the way I think they should be. Needing other people to be the ways I need them to be is my story to let go and may not be their truths.

Maintaining for me does not mean keeping people away from me that don't think like me or have emotions like anger or frustration. Maintaining for me is paying attention to my relationship with all emotions and thoughts so that I can connect with everyone as a being.

All these things were huge for me in order for me to come out of my cocoon. If I need the world and people to be a certain way to emerge, then I would never have been able to emerge. When I maintain my inner world, it allows me to let go of how the world needs to be in order for me to be okay because I am already okay.

MAINTAINING MY EMOTIONAL BODY

Breath Release for me is the most effective way to move my emotional history out of my cell tissue and create stillness in my body. In this beautiful place of stillness, there is peace and calmness. Unfortunately even though I know Breath Release helps me, I allow life situations to distract me. I put off doing what I know helps me. As you clear out emotional history, your body becomes light and calm. You will notice very fast when emotions are in your body. You do not notice in a judgmental or critical way; it's noticeable because you are now that aware of your body. I can only put off releasing for so long before it becomes a must in order to feel centered and calm again.

Since there is so much to discover about my emotional body, I created a chart as a tool. In the first column that goes down, I listed energies, and in the first row that goes across, I listed different areas of life. I'm constantly adding energies and areas of life. When I'm consciously working on my relationship with a particular energy, I will first sit in meditation and think about the energy and how I play with it in different areas of my life. I will type into each cell on the chart what I think my current relationship is with that energy. Do I allow this energy to flow through me in this area of life?

Do I judge this energy in others or myself? Does this energy bring up other energies in me? I gently, not judgmentally, look at how I play with different energies. This really helps me because in some areas of life, certain emotions are easy to navigate through, but other areas are challenging; it takes me consciously paying attention to my relationship with the energies to find my way through it.

	Yourself	Partner	Children	Parents	Friends	Acquaintances	Colleagues	Strangers	Work	Hobbies	Socializing
Love											
Hate											
Happy											
Sad											
Approve											
Disapprove											
Frustration											
Violation											
Respect											
Honor											
Disgust											
Rage											
Peace											
Inadequate											
Lacking											
Complete											
Important											
Worthless											
Value											
Coward											
Pain											
Accomplishment											
Reject											
Accept											
Lying											
Nurturing											
Trust											
Cheating											
Betrayal											

MAINTAINING MY ENERGY

I have a lot of energy. I can go and go and go and go, especially if I'm doing what I love. During the process of healing, cocooning, and rebirthing myself, I found it hard to stay busy enough to use all of my energy each day. Walking/jogging helps me greatly. When I feel too much energy in my body, I cannot focus, sit still, listen, or sleep well, so it's important for me to evaluate my internal energy levels. If I have too much energy in my body, it is hard for me to be around people. If I am around people, I feel all over the place and get overwhelmed quickly.

Maintaining Mentally

Mental maintenance is hard for me because my mind gets spun up very fast on stupid stuff. My favorite tool is asking myself constantly, "What do I need to do *now*?" I never ask what do I need to do next. What I need to do next is not important. What I need to do right now is important. Your being is intelligent enough that if this moment affects the next moment, it will tell you. I try to ask myself this at the end of each task or check in every hour when I'm struggling with being spun up with thoughts. Another interesting thing I would like to point out here is I've never asked, "What do I do *now*?" and not gotten an answer. If I try to project myself into a future moment and ask what is going to happen, I do not always get an answer or know what to do, but in the moment, I *always* get an answer and know what to do. There is a safe feeling in this truth.

It really is an amazing way to be powerful, keep myself out of time, and focused on this moment by asking myself, "What do I do now?"

MAINTAINING BY GOING WITHIN, NOT OUT

My answers and guidance always come from within. For example, if I'm walking down a dark street in a not-so-safe neighborhood and see a sketchy man coming toward me, I am *not* going to read him or his intentions. I'm going to go inside myself and ask if I'm safe in the now. Do I need to do anything in the now to be safe? I become very quiet and listen to the answer I receive, and then I act if needed. There is no situation where you will actually need to read the other person. What will always be more important is what you need to do *now*! Even if you read the person, it will most likely not help you because a lot of people feel weird, strange, or up to something. That will just scare you. What is always most important is asking, "What do I need to do right now?"

A SHIFT IS NEEDED

Something that was very hard for me while I was healing was other people's self-judgment. Now I'm strong enough to not give credit to other people's thoughts. Back then, when I was in the trenches of pain, it made me want to hide. Part of what I promised the world was "I promise I will create safe places to heal energies such as rage, violation, anger, helplessness, unfairness, and so on!" The reason I pledged this was because currently, our society has nowhere to heal difficult emotions. We numb emotions, we label emotions as negative, we move away from emotions, and we cut emotions off. We do not build a relationship with emotions, release emotions, and flow with emotions. This is a shift that our species needs in order to heal our emotional body and feel our connection to all that is. Compassion with yourself and others is needed as we break down old programming and release emotional history.

OUT OF THE COCOON

All of these inner tools helped me step back into the world again. It was exciting and different. I knew my intuition was significantly stronger, and of course I was curious to test it with Dr. Karen in the ED.

CHAPTER 10

Emerging

❖

IT HAD BEEN SEVERAL YEARS since I had been in the ED with Dr. Karen. My intuition had grown and changed so much in that time frame. I decided to go back into the ED and see if my speed and accuracy had increased.

I remember one time on the television show *Grey's Anatomy*, Meredith said something like, "Every patient is a liar until proven honest." This next story makes me think of that funny statement.

My first day back in the emergency department with Dr. Karen started in the doc box. Karen asked me, "Can you look at the lower right side of an older man's hip and tail-bone? The patient's name is Mike, and he is seventy-seven."

I told Karen what I saw as I was seeing it intuitively "Fractures! Several hairline fractures in the tailbone area! There is also a woman in the room with him, but I don't think she is in the physical form. His wife, maybe?" Karen scrolled through the patient's records, and under marital status, it read Widowed.

Karen added, "He fell two years ago and fractured his tailbone area. Is that what you are seeing, or are there new fractures?"

"They look new to me. I think he fell recently, but something strange is happening with my memory. When I'm in his thoughts, it feels like I'm missing sections of time. It doesn't feel like dementia or Alzheimer's. There are just blank spots in my memory, is the best way I know how to explain what it feels like," I said in answer to Karen's question.

"Okay, let's go see the patient," Karen said. She stood up, and we proceeded to the patient's room. During Dr. Karen's examination of the patient, Mike was very sensitive to touch, meaning when Karen touched him on his lower right side, during the examination, he would scream and jump in pain. Karen asked the patient twice, "And you're sure you didn't fall?"

Mike would answer, "No, no. I said no."

Karen ended the conversation with, "Okay, well, we will get a new x-ray and see what's going on in there."

I continued to follow Karen as she saw more patients. Between each patient's room, Karen provided me with the next patient's first name and age. If we were in a hurry, she would ask me an exact question. If we had more time, I would read the patient cold, meaning without any information. Then, with the information I had shared with her, we saw the patient for the first time. This gave Karen the opportunity to ask about anything I had intuitively seen. While she was talking to the patient, I stood quiet and listened. Hearing the conversation creates impressions within me. At the end of Karen's evaluation, if what I intuitively see is important, I will sometimes ask the patient a question or two.

For example, a patient came in with shoulder pain. He held his left shoulder much lower than his right. I symbolically saw several females standing on this man's shoulder. The pressure and weight he felt that they put on him was heavy, and it manifested physically. Out of the several women I noticed on his shoulder, one stood out stronger—his daughter. I could hear her nagging him and him being stubborn and refusing to move. After Karen was done examining him, I asked him if there was a chance he had a daughter. He said that he did have a daughter and laughed and said, "Why, do you know her?" Further stories followed, supporting what he perceived as pressure from his daughter, which was now manifesting as physical shoulder pain.

Most of the time, I say nothing to the patient and wait until we have left the room to share with Karen any additional intuitive hits I have seen. After seeing several patients, Karen and I headed back to the doc box where she entered notes, completed orders, and reviewed any test results and x-rays. When Karen reviewed Mike's x-ray, sure enough, there were new fractures in his tailbone area. Where the fractures where located would have been created most likely from a fall.

I started to read Mike again. His missing blank memory spots fascinated me, and I wanted to figure out what that meant. It occurred to me that I had not looked at Mike's largest energy loss. When I did, it showed me a significant energy loss out of his liver—what I would call an alarming energy loss out of his liver. And then it hit me! I started talking to Karen rapidly. "Karen, I know what is happening. I think he drinks alcohol. His liver looks like someone who drinks a lot of alcohol. Remember, I kept feeling like I was missing time. Maybe he drinks and passes out and doesn't remember falling?"

Karen added a liver test to Mike's orders. About an hour later, the results came back, and his liver results were elevated. Karen and I returned to Mike's room. Karen informed him that there were new factures on the x-ray. She asked him again if he might have fallen.

Mike again said, "No, no!"

Karen also informed Mike about his abnormal liver test results and that he needed to follow up with his primary care provider for further workup.

Mike asked, "Well, what could have caused something like this with my liver?"

Karen asked, "Is it possible that you drink?"

Mike answered, "I've never drunk a day in my life!" The patient continued to be adamant that he did not fall or drink, regardless of what medical tests were indicating.

Karen's medical opinion in this situation was this: "Although there are a few reasons for elevated liver tests, his results certainly suggested that he did drink alcohol, and his fractures are most consistent with falling. Based on what April was telling me, I agreed that he could have been lying about his drinking history and that he was possibly having blackouts and falling, resulting in his pelvis fractures. April's intuitive input helped explain Mike's presentation and clinical findings."

My first day back was amazing. I could describe in detail the patients' physical cell tissue, thoughts, emotions, and how to heal different parts of their beings. I was seeing a lot more than the last time I was in the ED. I understood more of what I was seeing, hearing, and feeling. My impressions were much clearer and more precise!

One time Karen asked me if a patient's hamstring muscle was torn.

I said, "No, it looks shredded to me. Like someone took a fork and shredded it."

When the ultrasound came back, the diagnosis in Western medical terminology is "torn hamstring," but when you look at the film it actually looks shredded and not torn. The point is that my intuition had gotten to a level of clarity that was an exact description of physical reality.

DAY TWO IN THE EMERGENCY DEPARTMENT

On my second day back in the ED, the story at the beginning of this book occurred. The aorta dissection case was different from the very start. Karen and I usually go see the patients after they are assigned to a room. This man was not assigned to a room but rather was sitting in triage behind a curtain. As Karen stated earlier, "The patient would have been put back in the waiting room." Of course the thought "I helped saved a person's life" was exciting. When Karen and I first started doing research, it was primarily to develop my intuition. As I did this, it taught both Karen and myself a lot. But the thought that I was actually using my intuition for something beneficial was huge at this point in my life.

The other cool thing I discovered was that I could look at the patient list on the computer screen and tell you which patient was the most severe. I was talking to a doctor named Jason. I noticed on his computer screen I was drawn to the patient who was in the most distress. I pointed at an older man's name on Jason's screen and said, "He needs the most help. He is very sick."

Jason looked at the list for a minute and said, "No, actually, this other guy is a lot more sick. He isn't going to make it."

I said, "Okay, let me rephrase that. The patient who is in the most distress that you can actually help is this man." I pointed at the same patient I did originally.

He thought a minute. "That's true!"

It was awesome being back in the ED and realizing how much my intuition had grown. I was also very discouraged as well in this area. Karen and I had done research on and off for ten years, and even though what we were doing was amazing, I still was not able to make a living as a medical intuitive. Even though I was helping save people's lives, could read people like a walking x-ray machine, could see all dimensions of the body, and could see how to heal the cause and not just the effect, the Western medical world considers this to be of no importance. It wasn't just me who was experiencing this. We currently have several powerful intuits and healers walking the earth. There is a man in Brazil who has healed thousands of people, but no one is researching him. In the United States, we spend millions of dollars on medical treatments that kill the body, treat only the symptoms, or numb the cause, but we spend little to no money on understanding the emotional body, energetic body, or the benefits of developing intuition. It is not understood yet that what I'm seeing and teaching is crucially important to health, evolution, and consciousness. I was beginning to learn that it didn't matter if other people hold what I do as important. It was not my business what other people viewed as important. What was my business was for me to listen to what intuitively I knew to be important. All of this happening was good for me, because it helped me look at what would actually help the human race the most. Intuitively the answer I received was to teach intuition and move the human race's understanding of the emotional body forward.

THIRD DAY IN THE EMERGENCY DEPARTMENT
The third day in the ED helped my contemplative mind find certainty and direction. Karen and I were in the doc box reviewing patients when an eight-year-old boy came in with a "severe migraine." As soon as I stepped into his energy, I started to get really hot—not a fever, but just my body was getting hot. Then I wanted to hold my head kicking and

screaming in pain. I felt super sick and almost vomited, and then I was fine.

Of course, Karen was just sitting calmly in her chair as I said all of this, and then she got up and said, "Okay, let's go see that patient."

Karen and I entered a dark ED room where both the boy's parents were present. Immediately the father started to describe to Karen what had happened. "About a year ago, he had a bike accident. He went over the handlebars and came down on his head. Ever since the accident, he has been getting headaches. We know when the headaches are coming because he always gets superhot first, and then the headache comes, and it lasts a few hours. He usually throws up, and then it's over. We have already been referred to a neurologist."

Karen asked questions and examined the boy. She ordered IV pain medication. Even though his headaches were not typical migraines, there was really nothing else that could be done in the ED.

As I listened to the father explain what he was witnessing, I could see within the child what was happening. He was reliving the bike accident over and over again. Once Karen was finished, I asked the little boy, "Are you having nightmares and seeing your bike accident in your head over and over again?"

I could see the little boy think a few seconds, and then he looked right at me and answered, "Yes, I am!" His parents gasped! They were shocked because they had no idea their son had been having nightmares and reliving this trauma. All of the sudden, it became obvious that he was not having migraines but was struggling with PTSD. He didn't need a neurologist; he needed someone to help him heal the story and his emotional body.

This case changed my life. I knew and understood how to help this little boy heal. Remember earlier, I told a story about John who had trauma at eight years old. He had debilitating migraines until he was thirty-two. The thought that this little boy didn't have to experience years of unnecessary migraines fueled me. It was becoming clearer and clearer how important it was for me to continue my research on the emotional body and to start to teach about it.

BEYOND COMPREHENSION

Karen and I had been living in our own little bubble doing research, but after the aortic dissection case, we were asked to lecture. I will never forget our first two-hour lecture to medical students and doctors. We gave several case examples of my impressions and then what the patients' test results indicated. At the end of the lecture, we asked for questions. Our first question by a doctor was, "So you're saying that you diagnose the patient before you ever go see them?"

Karen answered the questions because in that moment my mind was spinning. How in the world could you listen to a two-hour lecture and hear case after case where we describe doing this and then ask that question? This question haunted me for weeks. Not out of judgment, but out of sheer not understanding. Finally, I figured it out one day talking to Karen. After researching my intuition for ten years, Karen and I were used to it. It was normal to us, and like I said at the beginning of this book, "My intuition is like my arm!" It has always been there. For me, it would be like someone getting excited about my arm. For everyone else, this is beyond comprehension. The audience struggles to hear the case examples because they are stuck in trying to process the fact that humans are telepathic and empathic and see impressions that are accurate.

CHAPTER 11

What's Next?

❧

ONE DAY OUT OF THE blue, I received an email from a scientist friend of mine. He informed me that there was going to be a lecture given on medical intuition and wanted to know if I would like any of my work with Dr. Karen included in the presentation. Without thinking I answered him back and typed out exactly what stands in the way of humans recognizing their intuition and the medical-intuition industry moving forward.

The first thing I pointed out was unfortunately, we have very few people who can actually teach how to access intuition. Currently most medical-intuition courses consist of information about energy or data that has been created by true medical intuitives. You will be taught about the chakra system, and learn to diagnose *not* from intuition but from a chart that lists different ailments and the thoughts and emotions that create each ailment. Medical intuition has been reduced down to mind knowledge because very few people actually know how to teach someone how to access intuition.

Second, educated minds need to give this industry respect. It's that simple. We have such a resistance in our society to birthing anything new or outside of our mind understanding. At one time it was against the law in some countries to look at the inside of a body, to basically do surgeries. In modern times we have witnessed this with psychiatrists. I remember twenty years ago, you were referred to as a quack if you went to a psychiatrist. Now it's more common and respected as a crucial part of healing. Our society is not easy or gentle on new things being birthed. Thankfully we have people who refuse to give up who realize the importance of something before others do.

After typing the email, I realized that I had just answered my own "What's next?" questions. To move the industry forward, programs that teach access need to be created, and I need to find minds that are open. By "open," I mean not closed off to new ideas and advancement because of education. It's hard for educated minds to acknowledge that there might be greater wisdom then just what they have been taught in school. Although I'm complimenting them as magnificent beings who have vast knowledge of the universe, their mind knowledge tells them it trumps universal wisdom and stands in the way.

The truth is, I'm a connection teacher. I help people connect to their intuition and become powerful beings. There is no greater gift I could give the human race. Developing my medical intuition gave me credibility and proved that humans have more aspects of them then are currently being used, but now medical intuition was limiting me. I didn't just want to teach or support doctors in waking up to their intuition! No, I wanted to help the entire world wake up to its intuition and amazingness.

WHEN DID WE FORGET?

During this time I was also having an inner-ear issue. I would wake up at night, and it felt like my brain was spinning. It would make me so sick, I would throw up and couldn't walk or function until it stopped. As I lay in bed thinking about how sensitive these tiny stones (equilibrium) are in my ear that create balance, it hit me—oh, my God, we are brilliant beings. We completely form in our mothers' uteri without any thought. Our hearts beat without any thought. We breathe without any thought. Our circulatory systems work without any thought. We are some of the most complex, amazing organisms that walk this earth, and we believe that we do not have the knowledge to do this journey. *How stupid are we?* Really! I started to laugh hysterically at the ignorance. We insult ourselves by believing and teaching we do not know how to do this journey. When did we forget? We have been taught and are teaching that we do not know, and that simply is just not true. As beings, we contain everything needed to do this journey—even wisdom!

The only reason we started to teach or believe that we didn't know was to gain control and power. If you make a person believe that he or she needs you, then you have power. If you tell a person, "You have everything you need to do this journey already; go within and listen," then you would have no power over them. So we have reduced brilliant beings down to puppets on strings by teaching them that they "don't know." What would happen if we taught our children they contained the wisdom they needed to do this journey and how to access that wisdom? The evolution that would create with our species is exponential.

When I talk about this, it is interesting what comes up within people. One comment I heard from a person after reading this chapter was, "Well, we have to develop the mind!" In answer to that, I heard intuitively, "There is a difference between developing and programming." Currently we are programming because we want a certain outcome. We do not know that our children already have within them what they need to do this journey. We believe our learned mind knowledge knows more than the brilliant beings we are or the brilliant being standing in front of us.

THE ROAD TO FREEDOM

There was a time that humans fought and rose above physical slavery, but now the human race is waking up to the fact that we are enslaved by our thoughts. At first glance this may seem ridiculous, but upon further evaluation, you might conclude that believing thoughts has created a lot of suffering. When I read intuitively rapists, murderers, or even people who steal, it's because they believe their thoughts.

I'm never looking for what thoughts they were not taught that led to them doing these things. No, I'm looking at what thoughts did you believe that you acted on. If the person did not believe those thoughts, then the person would not have done what he or she did. The human race is just now starting to wake up and realize the power that believing thoughts creates. Believing thoughts has been the master of the human race for way too long.

What's funny about this is that the answer has always been right in front of us. Whether it is true or a parable, think about Adam and Eve when they ate of the tree of *knowledge* of good and bad. The human race's curse was *knowledge*. We didn't realize this was the point of the story. We have been fooled to believe that knowledge was advancing us, when in truth it is standing in the way of us accessing all wisdom.

How does knowledge stand in the way of all wisdom? Because every thought you believe creates an illusion of time. Even if you believe a thought about the moment, the moment had to have happened in order for you to think about it. The act of thinking is in the now, but what the thoughts are about always creates an illusion of time. The only access point to your intuition is the now. You cannot get an intuitive hit in a past moment or future moment. The intuitive hit happens and can only be experienced in the moment. If believing thoughts takes you away from the moment into time, then believing thoughts is taking you away from the access point to all wisdom.

CHAPTER 12

Brilliant BEINGS

⚜

FOR A LONG TIME, MY relationship with the emotional body stayed within my imagination. Imagination is the birthplace of intuitive ideas. The imagination is a beautiful well that bubbles forth creative ideas as thoughts, sounds, feelings, or pictures. Imagination is the *most* brilliant part of the human being. Imagination has no limit to what it can see, hear, feel, or know. Our memory, our intellect, is limited to what we can retain in a lifetime. For the most part, humans don't realize they are more brilliant than their learned/acquired knowledge. We think learned knowledge makes us more, when actually *believing* thoughts makes us smaller.

The reason believing thoughts makes us smaller is because the imagination is only experienced in the moment. The moment is the only access point. That is it; there are no other access points. Another word for the moment is space. There is a space where time does not exist, and that is the moment.

Every thought believed (not every thought you think, but every thought believed) creates an illusion of time. It makes you smaller because it moves you away from the access point to all wisdom, which is the moment.

When I talk about this, I always see the image of an adult holding up a nickel and a dime to a young child and then asking, "Which one do you want?" It's cute that the young child picks the nickel because it's bigger, not realizing that in our world of money, we have deemed the dime to be worth more even though it is smaller than the nickel.

In a similar way, the human race is doing this with knowledge versus the imagination. We have disconnected from the well, the very birthplace, of everything and have put a childlike worth on learned/acquired knowledge. I say "childlike" because our minds haven't been taught the significance of our intuition, and the mind only knows what it has been taught. To obtain information that is beyond what you have learned, find the place where all intelligence that exists resides—your imagination. You cannot get to your imagination in the space of timelessness if you are lost in the illusion of time that believing your thoughts creates.

This is why Albert Einstein said, "Imagination is more important than knowledge. For knowledge is limited, whereas imagination embraces the entire world." I guarantee you the brilliant ideas he birthed into this world did not come from his acquired knowledge. He told us where they came from, the *imagination*. Somehow we have completely missed the significance of this truth.

After working with me over the years, Karen made a profound observation about my intuition. She said that if I had gone to medical school or had taught knowledge about medicine, it would have gotten in the way of seeing my impressions and feeling my sensations clearly. I truly do not go to my knowledge, because there is none. In order to know all that is, I have to go to the well of imagination. It *was not* my learned knowledge that showed me impressions of a man's heart separating down the middle—no, that impression came from the unlimited well of the imagination. What I find amazing is that I know I am only touching the tip of the iceberg.

WHY THE EMOTIONAL BODY IS FORCING US TO EXPAND

When it came to researching and understanding the emotional body, there was no other place I knew to go than to my intuition, which ended up being the place I needed to go. The emotional body is not physical matter. It is a part of what creates physical DNA and is a nonphysical blueprint. This is very important because when humans are faced with answers they CANNOT get from learned knowledge, this forces us to expand.

Every human being has the ability to process all emotions, similar to a radio transponder being able to receive and process sound frequencies. Imagine if the radio transponder had the ability to reject, block, or suppress sounds within itself. Eventually the radio transponder would get weighted down and clogged up with sounds. Then it wouldn't work right, and eventually it wouldn't work at all. When new sounds try to come through, they back up behind the already held-onto sounds. This is the exact relationship humans currently have with the emotional body. We *do* have the ability to suppress (hold within us) emotions, and it is having catastrophic, detrimental effects on the physical body and our experience of life.

What causes human beings to suppress energy? We teach it energetically from conception, and then we teach it in behavior and programming once a child is born.

What do I mean by saying, "We teach it energetically from conception"? First, a parent's relationship with all energies has already played a part in determining the parent's physical DNA, which then also determines the baby's physical DNA. Second, how a mother responds when the energy of anger is in her body will teach the baby to respond in similar ways when the baby encounters the energy of anger. If a mother or father has a bad relationship with anger, he or she will teach this to the child energetically. A child will first learn how to respond to energies by how people around him or her respond to energies.

What do I mean by saying, "We teach it in behavior and programming"? We teach self-discipline and self-management from a very young age to be certain energies (love, kindness, giving, and compassion) but not to be other energies (hate, anger, frustration, or jealousy). Unfortunately, we do not teach how to process, understand, or flow with all energies. We are taught they are good or bad, even though you are *all* energies. This means you are taught that parts of you are bad, and you grow up believing that parts of you are negative or bad. This leads to everyone putting on a mask and pretending in life that we are only the so-called "good" energies, while hiding and suppressing the other parts of us that are the so-called "negative." In truth, there are no negative or positive parts of you unless you label them that way. It's futile for us to try and cut parts of us off or try not to be what we are. This is what I call emotional mutilation, and we teach it because we do it. It's a cycle within the human race that has been going on for eons. We are not here to lie to ourselves and pretend we are not certain energies that we are. We are here to master all aspects of our self.

This is also why so many people feel exhausted after socializing because it takes so much energy to pretend constantly. For a lot of people, it feels amazing to be alone where you can just be yourself. This is how not okay we have become with ourselves. Currently, self-love means only loving the so-called positive parts of you. The other parts of you are suppressed, blocked, rejected, or cut off.

Since this behavior has been happening for eons as a species, you can only imagine how loud the human race's emotional body has become. We suppress until we erupt. We do this as individuals—holding back and holding within us all kinds of emotions until every so often we explode, erupt, shut down, and/or hide. Each individual's emotional body collectively creates the emotional body of the human race. When the human race's emotional body erupts or explodes, we experience things like war and fighting.

Similar to a volcano or earthquake, we have had several small eruptions or plate movements to release pressure, but the buildup is alarming and will eventually demand our attention to survive. This is not uncommon in life forms to create evolving (change). When any life form is faced with suffering or survival, it adapts. The human race's emotional body roaring like it is will force us to adapt.

THE FEAR THAT BINDS US

A lot of human-based fears are caused because we have put false value on unimportant things. When I speak about telepathy, I notice fears in people. The thought of everyone being able to read each other's thoughts feels scary and even invasive. At this point in evolution, that would be a natural sensation because we live in a time in which way too much value is put on thoughts.

Earlier in the book, I mentioned that when people first meet me, they will sometimes be afraid I am going to read all of their thoughts. I laugh at this because I truly have spent a lifetime trying to let go of my thoughts. Why in the world would I want to read your thoughts?

Once a person realizes the impact that believing thoughts creates on health, our experience of life, and what we create, and that it is limiting us from accessing all wisdom, thoughts fall into their rightful places of being nothing more than dust without you giving them importance or power. You realize you are the powerful creator, and you are not a slave to thoughts anymore. You have freed yourself from the bondage of illusion. The last thing you will want to do is take on someone else's thoughts over being free.

It is hard to explain all of the changes we will experience as we wake up to more aspects of ourselves. I didn't say "new aspects" because these aspects have always been within us. Our minds are just becoming aware that we our brilliant beings. As we become more aware, *everything* will change.

TESTIMONY

***

I FIRST MET APRIL ABOUT eight years ago at a lecture she was giving on medical intuition in Encinitas, California. A mutual friend had posted the event, and it included a link to her website complete with her bio. I was naturally skeptical. However, when I read in her bio that she had done research at UCSD in the emergency department with Dr. Karen Van Hoesen, I instantaneously knew that she was the real deal. I was very excited to go to this lecture as I was fascinated with energy medicine and with energy profiling, of which I knew very little. But having worked in the medical field for close to thirty years, I had noticed patterns with patients' illnesses and knew there had to be something more to illness besides diet, exercise, and stress. What caused some people to have an illness, while others who by all accounts should have the illness but did not? Here was my chance to have many of my questions answered by someone who could read into the human body!

The day came to go to the lecture, and I was so excited as here was my chance to meet a medical intuitive in person! I listened raptly to April for two hours learning about medical intuition, and I even took notes. After the lecture, I was able to speak with April, and I knew she had a true talent that was unexplainable by traditional science. To my great delight, April had stated she was going to start teaching energy education classes and break down the human body into energetic systems and tie it into the emotional states and belief systems that we each hold.

April began teaching twice a week for only $5 a class! Each class went two to two and a half hours. What a deal to learn so much from someone with a gift such as this! I was hungry to learn and went to just about every class she taught. I took extensive notes. I began to compare what I learned in class with real-life patients at the hospital and with myself. I cannot even begin to tell you how accurate April is with reading into a person's energy field. It is beyond fascinating to watch her in action. During her classes is when I had the biggest breakthrough into my own personal psychology. April gave me the tools to do my own work. One of them being, when I am overwhelmed, taking a deep breath and asking myself, what can I do right now? As truly we only have the moment of now.

To this day, I continue to learn from April and from her unique perspective on energy and energy medicine. The wisdom and teachings she has brought forward are ahead of their time. One day, many will look back on her gift and her teachings in awe. April truly is a woman before her time. As for me, when I leave this planet and look back, April will have been one of the most influential people of my life.

—Mia Jones
San Diego, CA

FEEDBACK

Incredibly helpful and insightful! Always connects to the
situation and the POI (person of interest) accurately.
Thank you always!

❧

Read the energy, emotions, and situation very well!
Good suggestions! :)

❧

Excellent!

❧

First time caller, she read the people in my life perfectly.
Of course I was hoping the outcome would be different,
but she didn't try to sugarcoat the situation just to tell me
what I wanted to hear. Will definitely call again.

❧

Always a pleasure to speak with April Dawn!

❧

Picks up on situations that were really personal to that person. Amazing gift.

❧

April Dawn is great! She helped me understand a very confusing job interview. I knew right away she understood what happened, and I felt at ease I made the right decision to not accept the job offer. Thank you!

❧

Great! I think she is gifted and can tune in to people you ask about.

❧

She is incredible! Six months ago she told me that a guy I was dating had an addiction problem and that she didn't see me staying with him. I hung up on her because I thought she was 100 percent wrong. To my knowledge he had no addiction issue. Then one day he butt dialed me from a rehab center. I could hear him talking to someone about his relapse. She was right! After about another month of dating, I couldn't take it and broke up with him. Today our call was just as meaningful.

❧

Only way to describe April Dawn is amazing! She is the real deal. Give her a call. She connected with me and was able to see my situation. Thank you for everything. I will reach out to you in 2019 to give you an update.

❧

I really enjoyed talking with her! I was a little skeptical to be honest given it was my first time ever doing this, but she was spot on!

❧

Absolutely amazing! Thank you so much! OMG, I am blown away. So wonderful!

❧

Based on the actual messages and comments/mannerisms, she definitely connects. Definitely not one for fluffy conversations. Holding on to self-inflicted pain and suffering may stop one day. (Sigh). I've had a few readings over past few months. Details are always added, but the essence never changes.

❧

On point, direct, doesn't waste your time or money, and I have found April Dawn to be right every time!

❧

Absolutely amazing. She was able to connect with my mom and even used phrases and words my mom would use. Great reader.

❧

Honest and very insightful!

❧

Tunes in very well! Excellent!

❧

One of the best!

❧

First time calling...she totally tapped into the people in question...will definitely call her again. Thank you, April Dawn!

❧

April Dawn is amazing! Definitely give her a try. She will
tell you the truth whether or not it is good or bad,
but it's better to know either way.

❧

April Dawn is great to talk to about your situation and
answers all the questions you are not aware of!

❧

April Dawn was VERY informative, on point, and will give it
to you straight but in a kind and compassionate way.
I highly recommend her. :)

❧

April Dawn is the best! On target, direct, and accurate!
She is my go-to.

❧

She was very honest with me. It wasn't what I wanted to
hear because I have waited almost twenty years now for this
chance. However I have lived with it for this long; I can
continue with it as always. Thank you for your advice; she

was definitely able to connect with everyone. I would call her again. She was genuine.

❧

April Dawn is fantastic!

❧

Love this advisor. Not a lot of fluff—gets to the point. I feel she confirms connection well. Thank you.

❧

Thanks, April Dawn! That was incredibly helpful for me, and very accurate.

❧

Like her a lot—very strong in her skill.

❧

Thank you so much for your feedback and guidance on my journey. I appreciate your clarity into the situation. Blessings to you!

❧

Super spot on and detailed. Will call back for sure.

⚜

Always accurate, fast, and honest.

⚜

She was quick to pick up on the person in question
and read his feelings.

⚜

Great call! She was on the money with my questions asked!
I look forward to her predictions. I will definitely call again!

⚜

Thank you for sharing your amazing gift with me! Excellent
advisor!

⚜

Connected quickly and extremely well with my deceased
spouse. Gave messages in words and sayings he actually
used. Highly recommend.

⚜

Brilliant advisor! Very precise in elaborating the reasonings behind predictions that happen! Thank you for sharing your amazing gift with me!

🔱

Thank you so much. You always give details no one else could provide. Thank you.

🔱

She is THE real deal. She told me few months back that I would get a good job, but it will be temp; then the real one will show up, and THAT IS HAPPENING! Don't think twice; just call her, and she will impress you. THANK YOU, APRIL DAWN.

🔱

She was incredible. I'm not easily impressed, but I was really in awe of her abilities! Thank you!

🔱

She has a very unusual and special gift by being able to get into other people's minds and tell you what they're thinking. Totally amazing!

🔱

I enjoy speaking with April Dawn; her readings come to pass. I feel a sense of relief after I speak with her. Thank you so much!

❧

Thank you for your help and the information you gave me to keep moving forward.

❧

Always great. Past prediction happened.

❧

This girl is TALENTED. Wow—she is so deep and gifted. I'm dealing with a very tough situation, and she articulated it incredibly well. Major psychic ability!

❧

Thank you for another awesome accurate reading. Always help with moving things forward in the right direction.

❧

She nailed it!

❧

Thanks for a very good reading. It was short but very specific and gave a positive outlook and great advice as well.

❧

April Dawn was great! She told me the real story. Altogether it wasn't all I wanted to hear…but just may have room for potential. Even if it doesn't, she was great in how she handled my frugality, and she explained things well. Hopefully things can improve; if not I am ready to move forward with my life. Thanks, April Dawn!

❧

My apologies; my cell connection had cut off. Thank you dearly for your reading and assisting with my questions in my path. Loving blessings.

❧

THE BEST! Thank you very much!

❧

First-time caller. She is great!

❧

Past three years she has been a very accurate, fast reader. Very trusted advisor.

❧

April Dawn can really tap into someone very well! Thank you!

❧

Awesome as always. Accurate with even the things I choose not to share with anyone to see how well they are paying attention. LOL. Also very helpful guide when I hit low points and need guidance and encouragement. You rock, and I'm a regular. Thanks, April Dawn!

❧

Fast connection, very accurate when describing my situation, my POI, hope my job prediction comes to pass, and will definitely contact her again! I heard so many lies from $37 a min. "advisors." April Dawn told me the truth; hopefully things change in the future. Thank you!

❧

I was truly impressed with what we discussed, your ability to connect, and your quick responses! And you confirmed what I was feeling. Thank you!

❧

Amazing insight that helped me experience a miraculous breakthrough. April Dawn has a gift for reading below the surface and getting to the root of the problem. April Dawn, as you advised, I spoke to my inner child and focused on completely letting go. I felt myself falling backward and landing directly in God's arms with no fear, just comfort and peace. I woke up excited this morning and applied for the job for which I have been hesitant.

❧

What a gifted and talented woman. She got to the heart of everything, was honest and caring in her approach. She didn't sugarcoat things and was able to explain every situation in such great detail beyond what my fear/ego was telling me. I highly recommend her. Go direct to April Dawn as she is the real deal.

❧

Sorry I couldn't talk longer. Thank you for the short talk, and it does help. I feel better knowing that my own intuition on the matter is correct. It is what it is though. Heartbreaking, but real. Thank you for the honesty and quick connection.

❧

April Dawn is EXCELLENT! Details, timelines, and consistency. Wow!

❧

Thank you, April Dawn; you were great…you gave me peace. Can't wait for my next call to get answers from my wife. I miss her. Love, Jose. In loving memory of my wife.

❧

She's very helpful and correct! Won't waste your time. It's great to have a straight shooter on here.

❧

Thank you so much! You're such a beautiful soul and helping me and confirmed everything that I needed to know. I will contact you again soon! Beyond five stars!

❧

Thank you so much. I had a really rough week last week, BUT everything worked out. There are a lot of ppl. who love and truly care about me on the other side. Not only deceased relatives and spouse but higher beings.
I will definitely take your advice and try soothing things like yoga and meditation.

⚜

Thank you, April Dawn. Yes, I might be forced to leave here. I'm going to see if I can pay for everything myself first. You picked up on everything correctly; thank you!

⚜

Thanks. Reading was encouraging and was able to read the person like she knew him personally. Can't wait till September.

⚜

One prediction came true; I am confident that the other one will too! Thank you!

⚜

It's like he was sitting right there talking to him. I had been worrying and crying since his passing. He is the type of person that wants me to chill out and stop worrying so. The voices I hear from time to time was actually him. Stop spending so much money! Think of me as on vacation! Oh, my, stop crying! LOL. Was in fact him. We will be on vacation soon enough one day, but I'm taking both of your advice and focus on self and our daughter. She's the one that really needs me here. Closure isn't always given to you, and now I have to deal with it.

⚜

Thank you dearly for your energy, vitality, and love. I feel energized, powerful, and clear on my next steps. I appreciate your clarity and practical advice. You are a blessing! Smiles!

⚜

The message I received today from April Dawn was not necessarily what I wanted to hear, but it is what it is. Hopefully free will comes into play and turns out positive for me and my situation. So needless to say, she is accurate. Thank you!

⚜

She is terrific. If you're looking for someone that can communicate with someone that has crossed over OR is alive, she can talk directly to them and give you all of the answers you're looking for. She's spot-on accurate!

❧

She consistently gives specific details surrounding the situation asked and is very helpful. Amazing.

❧

I almost gave up on this entire platform until I called her. I appreciate you so much and look forward to learning more from you and checking out your book and materials.

❧

The most accurate reader on here. She is fast and honest. We have spoken now for almost three years, and I do not go to another reader anymore. I trust my readings with April Dawn. Thank you!

❧

Dead on! Thank you so much for your confirmation. I needed to hear this in order to move on from this person. Thanks again. Awesome reading. I will let you know how this plays out.

❧

You are amazing! She was able to answer each and every question had about ppl. That had passed away. I wanna cry so badly from joy, but it's almost like I can't. I never got a chance to meet my spouse's mom, and I wanted too so bad, especially after our daughter was born. I felt kind of cheated, but her messages to me today made it a lot easier to deal with her son. Thank you!

⚜

April Dawn is truly gifted and accurate. She was extremely detailed and was able to look closely at the situation in detail, which came through as accurate.

⚜

Wonderful. Great details.

⚜

Straightforward and really honest. We all need that. Thanks so much.

⚜

Amazing! Best reader on here by far. I've spoken with April Dawn for two years now, and EVERYTHING she has told me has come to pass. She is telepathic and will say things exactly like the person I've asked her about or even say exactly what they have said to me already. Her ability to talk to passed-over loved ones is amazing and shocking. From when I would receive an insurance settlement to what lot number our new home was going to be, she is right. She shocks me all the time with what she knows and how accurate she is.

❧

Fantastic reading, extremely helpful. Many times I did not listen to her warnings and was in trouble. I listen more to her predictions, no matter if it's bad or good. Because it was always accurate.

❧

Everything you said to me resonates, and I love that you were honest and gave me suggestions. Thank you very much.

❧

So crazy that you saw that there was a hiccup on our last call...and today it became clear what the hiccup was. I appreciate your insights and love that you always share the truth, even if it's not what we want to hear. It gives me the faith that when you do share the positive

news and see things, all the more reason to believe.
Thank you!

✤

The BEST accurate readings on here. We have spoken for
two years now, and all predictions have come true. She told
me my niece that passed over was with her grandmother,
and I thought that was impossible because she was in the
hospital. But I found out the next day my mom did pass,
and my niece was with her. Thank you!

✤

Thank you for your great insight and thoughtful advice.
Looking forward to prediction coming to pass.

✤

Wonderful reading, accurate and professional.
Highly recommend!

✤

Thank you for your great insight and information related to
my job search. I appreciate all the details.

✤

She is so tuned-in! Wow—a great reading, full of intense insight. Call April Dawn if you want the underlying truth!

⚜

She's the best.

⚜

Genuine insight. I've come to her over time with several different people, and she picks up on their unique personalities spot on! She is my number one go-to here. :)

⚜

April Dawn provided me with very accurate information about two people in my life! She's quick and succinct in the reading itself, but what she said really stuck with me for days afterward and gave me much to think about. Thanks, April Dawn!

⚜

She is amazing. Really good and honest.

⚜

Wonderful to speak to and always on point. Doesn't waste any time getting to reading.

❧

April Dawn is very compassionate and friendly. Would recommend her!

❧

Very helping reading tonight, picked up on situation in question and gave me the comfort I needed… accurate and great connection! Will call back for follow-up call.

❧

All I have to say is this lady is extremely gifted and so worth the money!

❧

Always positive and wonderful to speak to! April Dawn is very good with her readings! Highly recommend!

❧

April Dawn is amazing, honest, and to the point. I highly recommend; her readings have come to pass.

❖

Very nice and tunes in quickly. She's on point; thank you.

❖

Thanks for your insights. Right on track!

❖

WOW. That was amazing. You picked up on the personality of every person I asked about. Thank you for all of the information. It was very helpful. Have a great holiday.

❖

Always accurate, on point, and very truthful! Thank you soooo much!

❖

For 2017, I have called April Dawn, and she has been accurate with her readings. I have always enjoyed speaking with her, and her positive outlook is always welcomed. Thank you so much for being there for me through my

questions and readings. Highly recommend. Will
call back soon.

❧

Thank you for your guidance, insight, and perspective.
Today, I needed some clarity and direction,
and you helped quite a bit! :)

❧

April Dawn is a go-to when I want to know more about my
current situation. She's always straightforward
and connected.

❧

Thank you April Dawn! You are absolutely right about the
two people I asked you about. Thank you, and you'll be
hearing from me again.

❧

Every time I call, I get closer to fully understanding my destiny
and purpose. April Dawn helps me zero in on the areas that
count the most in fulfilling my heart's desires. Thank you!

❧

If anyone is thinking of calling April Dawn, please do. I always have a great reading, and she calls it as is. She gives you the truth and not just what you think you want to hear. Love you. xoxo

❧

April Dawn is amazing. She gets right to the heart of the matter. April Dawn provided insight that has given me confidence in moving forward with important career decisions.

❧

Always a fantastic reading! For the past year, all predictions and information have been accurate.

❧

April Dawn is always great to call to get a lot of information surrounding you. She picked up on all my questions and gave wonderful insight. I can now move forward with a plan.

❧

Thank you so much, April Dawn. It's always a pleasure getting readings from you. You're honest, encouraging, and truthful. Sometimes we don't want to hear what spirit has to say about our situations, but having someone to help us along the way is truly a blessing. Be blessed in all you do for the greater good and for spirit. Thank you again.

❧

I was not in a good place when I called, but you really helped me with excellent insight in order to move forward. Thank you!

❧

I love April Dawn. Been calling her for about two years on and off, and she is excellent. She will tell you how it is and tune in perfectly. Thank you!

❧

Excellent! Extremely accurate, wonderful insight!